NELSON'S WAR

NELSON'S WAR

❖

Peter Padfield

General Editor: Ludovic Kennedy

WORDSWORTH EDITIONS

First published in Great Britain 1976
by Hart-Davis, MacGibbon Ltd

This edition published 2000
by Wordsworth Editions Limited
Cumberland House, Crib Street, Ware,
Hertfordshire SG12 9ET

ISBN 1 84022 225 5

Printed and bound in Great Britain
by Mackays of Chatham plc, Chatham, Kent.

CONTENTS

May the Great God whom I worship, grant to my Country,
and for the benefit of Europe in general,
a great and glorious Victory,
and may no misconduct in anyone tarnish it;
and may humanity after Victory be the predominant feature
in the British Fleet. For myself, individually,
I commit my life to Him who made me,
and may His blessing light upon my endeavours
for serving my Country faithfully. To Him I resign myself
and the just cause which is entrusted to me to defend.
Amen. Amen. Amen.

NELSON, 21 OCTOBER 1805

Now, gentlemen, let us do something today
which the world may talk of hereafter.

<small>COLLINGWOOD, 21 OCTOBER 1805</small>

ACKNOWLEDGEMENTS

The photographs and illustrations in this book are reproduced by kind permission of the following. Those on pages 12, 34-5, 36, 38, 46, 66, 68, 71, 89, 93, 95, 100-101, 111, 114, 121, 126, 129, 132, 133, 136, 138-9, 140, 146-7, 150-51, 165, 168, 175, 179, 180-81, 183, 187, 190 and 192, National Maritime Museum; pages 42, 54, 56, 62-3, 112, 113, 120, 156-7, 170, 173 and 174, British Museum; pages 14, 32, 53, 117 and 189, Musée de la Marine, Paris; pages 17, 19, 186and 188, Portsmouth Royal Naval Museum, Victory Collection; pages 30, 33, 104 and 108, Greenwich Hospital Collection; pages 49, 81 and 134, National Portrait Gallery; pages 90-91, 128, 130 and 138-9,The Tate Gallery; pages 135, 140 and 194, Nelson Museum, Monmouth; pages 92, 159 and 177, Victoria and Albert Museum; pages 76-7, 125 and 184-5, courtesy of Richard Green (Fine Paintings); pages 40-41 and 131, courtesy of the Parker Gallery; - pages 50-51 and 89, courtesy of N. R. Omell; pages 162 and 193, The Mansell Collection; page 59, HMS Victory, Portsmouth; page 72, Inconographic Encyclopaedia by J. G. Heck 1851; page 87, Radio Times Hulton Picture Library; page 154, Willemöesmuseet, Assens; page 137, Portsmouth Royal Naval Museum, McCarthy Collection; and on page 166, courtesy the Hon. Mrs Llewellen Palmer. Illustration Research Service and Celia Dearing supplied the pictures. The maps were drawn by Bucken Ltd.

INTRODUCTION

THE OUTCOME OF THE 'GREAT WAR' of the nineteenth century – the titanic struggle between Europe under Bonaparte and Britain – determined the major boundaries which the twentieth century inherited. Britain, responding to the challenge of Bonaparte's 'Continental System', found herself, at the end of the struggle, in possession of the keys to the world's trade routes, vastly increased overseas markets, and all their wealth, while France's overseas trade and therefore her industry were correspondingly stifled by the British Naval Blockade

It was during the early years of the war that Britain asserted the naval supremacy that was eventually to prove decisive. In his exciting account of these years Peter Padfield has described the six crucial battles that make up the golden years of the Royal Navy. Throwing new light on these famous fleet actions, he shows that while they were remarkably unconventional, and, in their disdain for the enemy's usual formations, even apparently haphazard, they exhibited all the imaginative brilliance of their commanders, Howe, Jervis and, particularly, Nelson. A legend in his own lifetime but a very human legend, Horatio Nelson's genius and failings are central to the story, but Padfield also describes the hardships and sufferings on the gundecks, the outbreak of mutinies by British fleets at a crucial period in the war. Their resolution says as much for the heroism of the lowly paid British sailors as it does for the brilliant leadership of their commanders who were able to recapture their confidence and raise their morale to an unprecedented degree.

LUDOVIC KENNEDY

Prologue: Nelson's War

The period from 1793, when the revolutionary madness of the new French Republic drove her to war with Great Britain, until 1805 when Nelson died during the closing stages of his decisive victory over a Franco-Spanish fleet off Cape Trafalgar, can be seen in retrospect as one of the great turning points in history.

It was during these years that the Royal Navy gained for Great Britain what later French historians called 'The Empire of the Seas' – such a moral and operational ascendancy and chain of naval bases circling the world as to give her virtually unchallenged command of the oceans. This was the foundation on which nineteenth-century British industrialists, free-traders and free-booters raised the extraordinary edifice of the Victorian world Empire – and on which the nineteenth-century Royal Navy established the 'Pax Britannica'.

Trafalgar did not, of course, end the struggle which was to have such momentous consequences for the victors – in 1805 Bonaparte was still a tyrant and master of Europe, still determined eventually to invade and subjugate the British Isles. Yet it was the last and most brilliant fleet action of a series which won for the Royal Navy her supremacy, and which wrote a unique chapter in naval history. Before 1793 there had been few clear-cut naval decisions by comparison with the stalemates, partial victories and formalised promenadings that represented the norm in naval warfare. Nearly all real victories had come when one side or the other had been numerically far superior.

Then starting with 'The Glorious First of June', 1794, the Royal Navy, usually in inferior force, often ridiculously so, began taking on practically all the major European Powers allied or coerced against her by Bonaparte, gaining a succession of increasingly spectacular victories which made nonsense of all precedent and all the arithmetic of battle. Much of this was due to disorganisation and demoralisation among the opponents' fleets; much also was due to a series of outstanding admirals – Howe, Jervis, Duncan and Nelson – who combined resolution, competence and audacity to an extraordinary degree and who, between them, took fleet tactics as they had been known and shook them into something quite new and quite unique – the tactics of contempt. Finally, at Trafalgar, Nelson launched into the antithesis of any system of tactics – the contemptuous assault without order. Since Trafalgar was the last of the famous fleet victories and Nelson the highest embodiment of British naval genius there is a completeness about these years, 1793-1805, which demand, from this distance, that they be viewed as a series of battles in one outstanding war – *Nelson's War*.

NELSON'S WAR

Chapter 1

The Glorious
First of June

Sunday, 1 June 1794, commemorated in the battle honours of the Royal Navy as 'The Glorious First of June', dawned heavy with cloud over the French and English fleets in the Atlantic some four hundred miles west of Ushant. They were no more than eight miles apart, each formed in a more or less irregular line, ships pointing westward under easy sail, their bows plunging deep into a long and confused swell from the west, rising, showing an expanse of curved, greening copper below the waterline down to the keel itself as the piled water moved aft – lifted the ornate sterns – and the bowsprits dipped again until the sea pounded up in a flurry through the head gratings. The wind drove across the swell from the south, bending topmasts and t'gallants to starboard, tautening the weather shrouds, sighing through the rigging and clacking blocks.

The southernmost, therefore windward, force of twenty-five sail of the line was the British Channel Fleet commanded by Admiral Lord Howe – 'Black Dick' to the men on account of his dark and serious countenance – to his officers a tactician of originality, a perfectionist in fleet handling, the first sea officer of the day. At the main peak of his flagship, the 100-gun first-rate *Queen Charlotte*, he flew the Union Flag normally reserved for an Admiral of the Fleet.

Downwind in more extended formation after the night's station-keeping, the French fleet numbered twenty-six of the line under Rear-Admiral Villaret de Joyeuse. Villaret was more than twenty years younger than Howe; although a brave and accomplished officer who had learned his business under Suffren, one of the most skilful fighting admirals of the pre-Revolutionary French service, he had lacked the patronage to rise higher than lieutenant until the Revolution thinned the ranks; soon those Royalist officers who were not imprisoned, guillotined or strung from lamp-posts during 'The Terror' had fled the service, and in 1794, one year after the forces of revolution had turned outwards against the monarchies of Europe who had allied themselves against the French Republic, Villaret quite suddenly found himself in command of the Brest Fleet. So far the fleet's performance had been lamentable. With the old professional officer corps broken up and the gaps filled with merchant skippers unused to the disciplines and different skills of a fighting service or by Republicans whose mouths proved larger than their abilities, with ships' companies encouraged to insult – even in some cases dismiss – their officers, and with the shore administration in similar chaos, the ships had scarcely put to sea. The two short cruises made had been disastrous; collisions,

Admiral Lord Howe ('Black Dick') in the judgement of many, the first sea officer of the day.

13

Rear-Admiral Villaret de Joyeuse, whose task at the First of June was to prevent Howe's fleet from falling on a vital 'American' convoy.

dismastings and wholesale disobedience had culminated in flight from a numerically inferior British fleet.

The British had not used this period of their enemy's utter confusion to the best advantage. Neither the Prime Minister, the younger Pitt, nor his cabinet had wanted war, and when they were forced into it by the French Revolutionaries' urge to external conquest – rationalised as an aim to bring the benefits of republicanism to all peoples oppressed by monarchy – they had lacked the drive or the strategy, as at first they had lacked the means, to crush the young Republic. The British Army was minute by continental

14

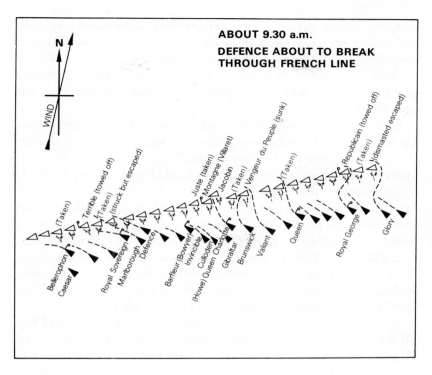

ABOUT 9.30 a.m.

DEFENCE ABOUT TO BREAK
THROUGH FRENCH LINE

N

WIND

Bellerophon (Taken)
Caesar
Terrible (towed off)
(Taken)
(struck but escaped)
Royal Sovereign
Marlborough
Defence
Barfleur (Bowyer)
Invincible
Culloden
(Howe) Queen Charlotte
Juste (taken)
Montagne (Villaret)
Jacobin
Gibraltar
(Taken)
Brunswick
Vengeur du Peuple (sunk)
Valiant
(Taken)
Queen
Republican (towed off)
(Taken)
Royal George
(dismasted escaped)
Glory

Map 1
Opening of the Glorious
First of June, 1794.

standards, less than fifty thousand men, some two-thirds of whom
were dispersed in separated overseas garrisons. Britain's strength
was in her Navy, her sea trade and the wealth that flowed from
trade. Her Navy totalled some four hundred warships – 140 of the
line – against a French total of under 250 – less than 90 of the line –
and almost by reflex Pitt and his Ministers turned to a maritime
and overseas strategy, aiming to use superior naval strength to cut
off and seize French colonies and bases overseas, both to cripple
French trade and to increase that of Britain, using the additional
wealth to keep armies from the other continental monarchies,
chiefly Prussia and Austria, in the field against France.

Although the policy had served Britain well earlier in the
century – brilliantly under the first Pitt during the Seven Years
War – it was not calculated to bring quick results. And as it was
early compromised by the differing ambitions of the monarchies
allied against France, and by the need to send British troops to the
continent to save Holland from falling into French hands, and
other subsidiary adventures which were never co-ordinated into
a decisive strategy, France was given time. She used this to good
effect on land, although not at sea, where her ill-disciplined and

15

ill-found fleets allowed the British total command; colonies dependent on naval links with the mother country were seized; disdainful British frigate captains chased and outfought French cruisers, disorganising all French carrying trade and reinforcing a moral supremacy which the British service had long assumed, and now found indisputable.

By 1794 France's situation was desperate. Trade disruption had been augmented by disastrous harvests and parts of the country faced famine unless a convoy of nearly 120 ships from the West Indies and American ports, many loaded with grain, could be fought through the British command of the oceans. This was Villaret's task. What he and his captains lacked in experience, they were to make up for in revolutionary ardour; to ensure it the People's Commissary charged with the administration of the Navy was sailing in Villaret's flagship *Montagne*, as joint commander of the force. To make doubly certain Villaret had an assurance from Robespierre himself that if he allowed the great convoy to fall into Lord Howe's hands he would answer for it with his head.

So far Villaret had done all that could be expected. He had kept all but one of his raw captains together when Howe had sighted, given chase and attacked his fleet on 28 May, and in running he had drawn Howe from the convoy rendezvous position. On the next day, he had formed and manoeuvred his line skilfully against Howe's attempts to break through from downwind. And although Howe had succeeded in cutting it and isolating the rear ships, he had worn around with the rest of his fleet promptly enough to save them from capture – although not from such a severe mauling that two had to make for home. In rescuing them he had lost the position of initiative to windward, but as his aim was not to force battle, but merely to save the convoy by drawing the English fleet away, this was not a great disadvantage – indeed it was the best berth for a fleet intent on orderly retirement.

The following day, 30 May, a thick fog had descended over both fleets and had lasted long enough to prevent an English attack on the 31st. Meanwhile the wind had remained favourable for the convoy, which passed close but out of sight, and was now some way south and east of them on its way to Brest. Villaret had no means of knowing its exact position; in any case the slow and unwieldy mass of merchant ships would be an easy chase for Howe for several days. His duty therefore – and his neck – required him to stand up to the attack he anticipated and do sufficient damage to Howe's ships, particularly in their masts and rigging, to prevent them catching the convoy afterwards.

Round shot, bar shot and grape shot.

Howe had even less knowledge of the convoy's whereabouts than Villaret, but his task was equally clear. The English strategy for trade protection and attack on enemy trade rested on neutralising the main enemy battle fleets, either by containing them inside their harbours with the English fleets riding outside – known as 'close blockade' – or by enticing them out and destroying them at sea – 'open blockade'. With the enemy main fleets out of action one way or another, English convoys could be protected and enemy convoys plundered by small squadrons of 'line' ships or frigates. Howe was a believer in 'open' blockade, and in this cruise after the American convoy he had deliberately left the way clear for Villaret to escape. Now that he had found him, he meant to destroy him.

The difficulty was not that Villaret had twenty-six sail of the line to his own twenty-five, nor that his opponent's best ships were generally larger, better proportioned and more heavily gunned than his own; none of these things counted, for the greater discipline and rapidity of fire from the British guns' crews invariably gave them the advantage over Frenchmen once the ships came to close action; moreover the British method of waiting, usually lying prone on deck, until they were close enough to unleash double-shotted broadsides laid for a horizontal trajectory into the enemy gun decks to kill, maim and drive the enemy gunners from their pieces, 17 had proved throughout the century a more effective battle-winner than the usual French method of firing from a distance and aiming high to destroy masts and rigging and immobilise their opponent's ships. This had been pointed out by the French tactician, Morogues, thirty years earlier:

> The enemy, by skilfully waiting till the impatient ardour of our first fire, we so much boast of, gradually subsides, gain the advantage of conquering us in the end, which a steady and well-timed, as well as an unremitting fire never fails to procure them.

Nevertheless the French habit of distant and high fire, combined with skilful withdrawal by gradually falling off downwind, thus keeping outside effective range for the British method, had posed almost insoluble problems for British admirals manoeuvring in the orthodox way to form a 'line of battle' parallel to the enemy line, thus bringing all guns of the broadside to bear. During the peace before the outbreak of the Revolutionary War a new school of British officers, Howe among the leading lights, had sought ways of preventing the French withdrawals; as a result of the exercises practised then, Howe had added an entirely new manoeuvre to the Instructions which he issued to his fleet at the outbreak of war in 1793. It was unlike anything that had been tried in the century and a half since 'line of battle' had emerged from the group mêlées of earlier times; it involved the fleet having the windward position sailing down on the enemy almost in line abreast, but each ship angled – thus a line of bearing – and each cutting through the enemy line close astern of her opposite number, then rounding up parallel and close on the *lee* side of her opponent, preventing her falling off downwind – *holding* her to close action.

It was a bold manoeuvre carrying immense risks; every ship in her almost end-on approach to the line of enemy broadsides would be raked without means of reply until she broke through; damage to masts and rigging during this time might render her unmanageable and frustrate the design, while for those which did break through there was the danger of firing into each other as they sought to rake the enemy either side. Besides all this, the windward position Howe was proposing to forego had always been considered the position of advantage. Clearly the tactic could only have been devised for a service absolutely confident of its superiority in close action by a man who had weighed the risks from very practical experience.

Howe's experience in close action was second to none; his name was a byword for holding his fire until practically alongside the
enemy; as captain of the *Magnanime* in Hawke's fleet at the Battle

of Quiberon Bay, 1759, perhaps the most spectacular naval victory of the century, he had chased to within pistol shot of *L'Heros* before giving her the first broadside of an encounter which the French survivors described afterwards as 'a massacre rather than an engagement'. In the same *Magnanime* he had led the line in an attack on a fort near Rochefort, standing on in perfect silence through the enemy shot until within forty yards of the walls, when he had dropped anchor and 'began so terrible and incessant fire that the ship seemed to be one continuous flame. In about an hour's time the Governor struck his flag, when the smoke clearing away, discovered not a fort, but a confused heap of rubbish.'

Such was the man who commanded the British fleet, himself an epitome of the British method, but also – and this was not typical of the British tradition – a thoughtful and imaginative tactician, one moreover who took the greatest pains to exercise his ships until they could form and manoeuvre to his signals with the utmost precision and rapidity in all conditions. A French prisoner on

Flexible rammer and sponge; also cartridge and leather cartridge case.

board one of his ships expressed astonishment at the speed with which the British ships were tacked; five minutes against fifteen for his own fleet.

Despite his own excellence Howe had great difficulty in expressing his ideas to his captains. Naturally shy, even awkward with those he did not know, and with a curious manner of speaking in involved, dependent clauses, he inspired respect but often little understanding. Despite the brilliance and originality of his new manoeuvre of breaking the enemy line *in every part*, many of his captains did not appreciate its significance and some did not even understand the meaning of the signal directing it. For his part, Howe did not have confidence in all his captains; too many, he thought, had obtained their commands through patronage without merit.

As for the men of his fleet, they trusted him, despite his first appearance of harshness and austerity and deep reserve, as a man of genuine compassion who had their interests at heart. They knew that the sick and maimed in his ship were provided with fresh meat and other delicacies from his personal stock, that after an action he made it his business to go below and sit and talk with each wounded man individually. 'Black Dick' was also 'The Sailors' Friend'. This was by no means typical of all British officers.

Even more remarkable, in his advanced years when caution ought naturally to have replaced the fire of youth, was his willingness to take risks to inflict crushing defeat rather than simply drive the enemy off with orthodox 'line' tactics – especially as in this case he was worn out from four days of manoeuvring and constant vigilance.

> Some occasions in our profession will justify if not require more hazard to be ventured than can systematically be defended ... But admitting the risks of mutual injury to be as great as I believe many officers supposed, the times or peculiar circumstances of the country ... called loudly, in my opinion, for some conclusive issue of the contest ...

As the sun climbed between the banks of cloud around the horizon, brightening the topsails of the French ships which were closing their lines to meet the expected attack, Howe steered a northwesterly course towards them. The wind was fresh on his quarter, the best point for sailing, and by seven o'clock he was within four miles, still well outside extreme gunshot but, with such a wind, within easy striking distance. He turned the fleet westerly together to sail parallel with the French, close-hauled on the larboard tack, and dressed the line with his usual care. At 7.25, satisfied with his captains' efforts, he signalled the mode of attack:

numeral pendants 34: 'Having the wind of the enemy, the Admiral means to pass between the ships in the line for engaging them to leeward.' To make sure that all ships took in the signal a gun was fired as the bunting broke. Yet, uncertain how many of his captains would have the resolution to obey, or in some cases the intelligence to understand his intention, he confided a prediction of the result to his First Captain (Chief of Staff), Sir Roger Curtis: one French ship would be taken for every British ship that broke the line.

Meanwhile the hands were piped to breakfast. Galley fires had been extinguished long since, and benches and mess tables stowed below; it was a cold meal of gruel and biscuit eaten on deck between the great guns beside the handspikes, rammers, sponges, worms and other instruments and ammunition laid ready to serve them. They had eaten like this for some days; now, animated by the sight of the deep red enemy hulls close to leeward, their rows of open gunports and gun muzzles showing clearly, excited by the impending action and supremely confident of triumph, they swapped sanguine predictions, boasts or macabre jests, gave instructions about the dispersal of articles in case they were killed, fell silent or indulged in senseless bravado according to temper, experience or state of health.

Many were debilitated. Scurvy was still a scourge of cruising fleets and although there were no specific cases as yet, the early stages of the disease took many forms; languor and apathy were the most consistent symptoms. Besides this, rheumatic fevers, chronic chest complaints and catarrhs brought on by the dampness between decks, wet hammocks and bedding, wet, unchanged clothes and personal carelessness due to fatigue and ignorance, were common. A number of men suffered from venereal complaints and many more from strains and ruptures caused by a combination of strenuous duty and unbalanced diet; heaving enormously heavy casks of water and provisions, cannon and carriages, grappling canvas and hauling on tackles with abdominal muscles weakened by vitamin deficiency took their toll even in the predominantly youthful crews; every seventh or eighth man wore a truss for hernia.

And yet the majority responded to the prospect of action with eagerness. It was a way of forgetting. It provided a break in the harsh monotony of cruising – a wild break, terrible beyond words, and many of those discussing the prospects on this bright Sunday morning were destined to end the day permanently deranged, and end their lives in asylums. But it was a break and most were careless of the consequences. Inured to constant hazard from a very early age, with a fierce pride in their reputation for courage, they possessed, in the words of a fleet surgeon who knew them intimately, 'a degree of contempt for danger and death that is to be met with nowhere else'. After a century of more or less continuous warfare with the French they were also arrogant in their own superiority, their triumphant character as British seamen; 'they considered themselves at sea as rulers by birth-right'.

After breakfast they stood to their quarters. The guns' crews had gay coloured or black silk handkerchiefs bound around their heads over their ears to shut out the worst of the deafening blast of the cannon, and another handkerchief or scarf about their waist over white duck or blue or striped cloth trousers. Their chests were bare. Among them were Marines who had stripped off their tunics and stowed their arms amidships together with the long steel-tipped boarding pikes and sharpened cutlasses placed handy for the boarding parties. Other Marines in scarlet uniform with muskets and bayonets were stationed on the poop, others along the gangways connecting the forecastle with the quarterdeck, together with 'waisters' whose duty it was to work the ship. When all were assembled, checked by lieutenants and midshipmen who between them supervised all sections of the gundecks, each ship's captain, followed by a retinue of officers, made rounds of inspection, repeating phrases of encouragement as they went, applauding determined responses, and growled requests to lay them close alongside, reinforcing an electric spirit of eagerness to close and conquer.

A few minutes before 8.30 Howe ordered a preparatory signal for each ship independently to steer for and engage her opponent in the enemy's line. Taken together with the previous signal '34' his intentions should have been clear: each captain was to put up his helm and steer for his opposite number and, instead of rounding up to engage from to windward, pass through the line under her opponent's stern to luff up close in her lee. Some of the captains did not appreciate this, simply taking the latest flags as an instruction to go down in the time-honoured way; others regarded signal '34' as permissive – allowing them to engage from windward or leeward as they thought best in the circumstances. Others again understood clearly and resolved not to flinch from the attempt.

At 8.38 the preparatory flag above the hoist was hauled down smartly and a gun fired. One by one the great double steering wheels on each quarterdeck were turned by teams of quartermasters; ropes creaked through tiller blocks below, the massive helms swung ponderously to larboard. Simultaneously groups of quick men by the quarterdeck belaying pins for the mizen rigging worked almost by reflex, throwing off the turns around the pins, slacking the bowlines and lee braces which kept the mizen topsail sharp into the wind, hauling on the weather braces to shiver the canvas, releasing the pressure aft, allowing the pulling head sails to help the rudder swing the bows downwind. Other groups stood by the bowlines and braces for the fore and main topsails to trim the sails as the ships paid off. Others were high aloft along the upper yards preparing the t'gallant sails.

So the fleet swung together from line ahead into line of bearing and once again ran down towards the enemy line, each ship steering for a point ahead of her opponent as the French, still close-hauled on the larboard tack, were making way slowly through the water. The English ships with the wind on their larboard quarter swelling the topsails, jibs and staysails out in lovely curves, drove across the clean, deep blue swell at some five knots in perfect order 'as if we were calmly coming to anchor'. The sun flashed from the panes of the stern galleries, gleamed on the wet yellow and black sides and masts, struck shadows of spars and rigging, blocks and sails across stretched white canvas and sanded decks. Captains with their first lieutenants and aides leaned against the heel of their quarterdeck or paced with studied nonchalance – anxiously alert nevertheless for any shift in the relative positions of their near consorts, eyes lifting to the sails or the flagship's halyards, or gazing through the starboard rigging at the one enemy they were steering for, judging whether they were holding her on a sufficiently steady bearing to fetch her close. Absorbed as they were, another part of their minds filled with a sense of the scale and grandeur of the scene. 'I do not think there could have been a more noble sight than seeing twenty-five British line of battle ships intending to pass through the French line of twenty-six.' Each man was lifted out of himself, member and partner in stirring events far greater than himself. 'Down we went under a crowd of sail, and in a manner that would have animated the coldest heart, and struck terror into the most intrepid enemy.'

Howe, sweeping the line with his telescope from the high poop of the *Queen Charlotte*, noticed that the seventh ship on his larboard bow had set t'gallants over her topsails and was drawing ahead of the rest. 'Look at the *Defence*,' he exclaimed, 'see how nobly she goes into action!' Then, as the *Queen Charlotte* herself drew ahead of her immediate neighbours on both sides, he had them signalled to make more sail. One of them, *Culloden*, which had backed her mizen topsail so as not to shoot ahead of her next to larboard, now filled and set her foresail and foretopmast staysail as well, soon pulling so much ahead of her station that she came up between the 23

Barfleur, flagship of Rear-Admiral Bowyer, and the enemy. The admiral hailed her with his speaking trumpet to keep clear of his line of fire. The *Culloden* hauled up her foresail and backed her main and mizen topsails until she had fallen back.

Several other captains had one or more topsails aback by this time as they tried to meet the conflicting demands of keeping station with their consorts and with their flagship and at the same time steering towards their opponent. The irregularities increased as they closed within long gunshot, something over half a mile, and the French opened with high, ranging shots from the head of the line first, the English van division and particularly the *Defence* and *Bellerophon*, flagship of Rear-Admiral Pasley, having closed faster than the centre and rear. Those captains who had misunderstood Howe's intentions or lacked the resolution for close action lagged; at the extreme western end of the van division, the *Caesar*, usually one of the faster sailers, hung back most conspicuously with her main topsail flat aback against the mast and no other sails set. Meanwhile those captains who had determined to break the line had set more sail, the sooner to pass through the zone of fire.

In the centre the *Queen Charlotte* was ahead of her division and making for Villaret's huge flagship, *Montagne*. Howe, after signalling all the laggards to make more sail, directed his First Captain to have the signal prepared for closer action, remarking that he only wanted it in case of captains not doing their duty. Then, turning to the officers about him, he closed the little signal book he always carried. 'And now, gentlemen, no more book, no more signals. I look to you to do the duty of the *Queen Charlotte* in engaging the French admiral. I do not wish the ships to be bilge and bilge, but if you can lock the yardarms, so much the better – the battle will be sooner decided.'

Despite his intention to have done with signalling, the impression that a few of his captains were not supporting the leading ships as they might soon led him to call for the signal for closer action; this was followed by a general signal to all ships to make more sail. The *Charlotte* herself had set her foresail by this time and her t'gallants in an effort to close the *Montagne*, which was making a good deal of leeway from them.

Soon the fire grew heavier and spread from the head of the French line towards the centre; it was taken up by a few ships in the rear as the two flagships of the British rear division, the *Royal George* and *Queen*, outstripped the rest. Few of the British ships outside the foremost of the van division had replied yet although some had fired guns to cover themselves with smoke. In the centre division Cuthbert Collingwood, captain of the *Barfleur*, now under fire from two French ships, remarked to his admiral, Bowyer, that their wives would be going to church about this time. It was approaching ten o'clock. 'But I think the peal we shall ring about the Frenchmen's ears will outdo their parish bells.' The *Barfleur* held on in silence, both men determined not to open their broadside before Howe – 'and he is not in the habit of firing soon'.

Most of the French shot went high. For the British guns' crews lying at their quarters on the damp, sanded decks, the flight of the balls sounded like tearing canvas overhead; thuds or concussion of metal on metal or jangling blocks hardly louder than the noises from the wind and working timbers, told of shot ploughing through a yard or mast, breaking up fittings, cutting rigging. Occasional louder, rending crashes followed by the low whirr and thud-thud-thud of innumerable oak splinters, men's shrieks, groans and oaths betokened hulling shots. The first trickles of blood made patterns in the sand down towards the lee scuppers.

The men lay tense with set expressions as the wounded were carried to the hatchways and down; they exchanged observation and rumour in tight whispers, those on the upper decks peering out of the lee gunports. Each time a roll brought them lower the French line filled the small space above the bulk of the cannon; with the nearest ships inside five hundred yards they stretched away into the distance, five miles from van to rear, wallowing and pitching to the swell, spray splashing up the curved timbers, puffs of white or grey smoke swelling from the ports in ragged patterns, rising to cover the hull and lower masts so that the topsails and t'gallant masts and the white ensigns with the tricolour in the corner appeared riding on sunlit clouds; then the wind shredded the clouds astern, and from some of the ports men could be seen scrambling out, sitting astride the guns to sponge and load – a practice discontinued in the British service for over a hundred years.

The first British ship to break the line was the *Defence*, seventh in the van division. She had reserved her fire till very close, perhaps two hundred yards, then on the order passed down from the quarterdeck the men of the starboard batteries had risen like tigers roaring huzzas which carried with terrifying clarity over the intervening water, and waiting for the roll to bring the cannon horizontal, had unleashed a double-shotted broadside straight into the deep red hull of the ship astern of their intended opponent. The cannon leaped back until brought up by the breeching ropes, and the men jumped into their loading drill, rehearsed so often that it 25

Engagement of the
Royal George and
Majestic during the first
stage of the Battle of the
First of June.

27

was second nature, gasping and choking in the smoke still spreading from muzzles and vents.

On the lower deck the ports were dropped to keep out the waves which had already surged in and swept parts of the deck clear of sand. Sheepskin sponges with flexible rope handles were dipped in the half-casks of brine placed by each gun and thrust in the muzzles down to the breech end to douse any remnants of fire; other men took a paper cartridge of measured powder from a powder boy and·stood ready to place it in the muzzle directly the sponge was withdrawn; powder boys hurried to the damped furze screens around the midships hatchways to collect replacements from the hands stationed to pass cartridges from the magazines; at the guns flexible rammers were used to thrust the cartridges down to breech ends, then the balls, weighing thirty-two pounds on the lower deck, eighteen pounds on the deck above, were rammed home, two to each gun – or one ball and one canister of grape shot – with a rope wad to keep them from rolling out. Each gun captain, having pushed a priming wire down the vent at the breech end to pierce the cartridge, filled the vent with fine powder from a powder horn or a quill tube, leaving a little heap at the top, cocked the flint-lock and held the firing lanyard loosely; handspike men levered up the breech end so that the wedge (quoin) on which it rested could be re-set for the angle of elevation needed for a horizontal fire just skimming the wave tops. The men assigned to the side tackles to haul the gun outboard again took the strain. Port lids were lifted. The tackle men heaved. The carriage careered out with the heel to smack against the port sill. Gun captains crouched, peering along from the breech rings past the swelling metal at the muzzle to the enemy hull, wet and bright and so close that the scores of holes from the first broadside could be seen clearly, tapped one side or other of the breech as a signal for the handspike men to lever the carriage that way, stepped back to the full extent of the firing lanyard, still stooping, waited as the ship rolled, yawed – then as the muzzle came in line with the enemy ports, jerked the line. Flints sparked; vent fire leaped to the deckhead beams; cannon cracked in irregular sequence filling the low space with intermittent, confined thunder, shaking the frames and deck beams throughout the hull as they jumped and brought up clattering against the breeching ropes. The men, half stunned by the concussion, choked in the smoke, swept up in the red fever of battle, roared more huzzas as they heard the last of the balls smashing through the enemy timbers with a sound like the breaking down of a dozen doors.

As the loading sequence recommenced, the *Defence* swept through the line, and the larboard guns – foremost first, the fire gradually spreading aft – poured their shot through the timbers and window frames of their opponent's stern. As the balls were heard thudding from end to end of the enemy gun decks, sudden shrieks of the wounded were borne on the wind. At the same time the Frenchman was under fire from the *Marlborough* – next on the larboard side – as she pressed on sail to break through the line just ahead. Some of the *Marlborough*'s shot passed over and into the *Defence*'s rigging as she rounded up close in the French lee. The other ships of the van division which had borne the brunt of the earlier days' fighting and had suffered aloft failed to break through, but – with the exception of the *Caesar* which held back at long gunshot – each closed to within some two hundred yards of her opposite number before luffing into the wind and pouring in broadsides from the windward berth. The French gunners, unskilled and partially exhausted as they were from their earlier fire, replied with spirit.

Dense banks of smoke wreathed the head of the line; bursts of flame from gun muzzles flickered through, noticeably more often from the British ships. Holes appeared as if clawed out of the topsails, rigging fell slack, masts staggered as the ships pitched, or fell carrying a tangled web of ropes and spars and bellying canvas; below in the smoke and fearful din, balls and splintered oak or shivered metal tore through flesh and muscle and bone, spreading death and agony. The sanded decks became tacky with blood. Wounded were carried below to the surgeons' dim and shaking platform where those who had undergone operations in the earlier days' fighting encouraged those about to suffer the ordeal with only strong spirits to blunt their senses, and a leather pad to bite on as the nerves were cut and the teeth of the saw grated through bone. On the gun decks the remains of those fortunate enough to have been killed instantly were bundled through the ports into the sea – or on the French ships simply hauled out of the way and left in heaps amidships, or flung down into the hold. Survivors of depleted guns' crews took over the duties of the missing. Officers encouraged with huzzas or drew their swords and threatened the cowed and shocked back to their duty; midshipmen helped at the most depleted guns. Those with the most heavy work were more fortunate than the youngsters waiting with cartridges who had time to glimpse the mutilated and hear their cries – and think. Those straining at the sponges, rammers and tackles had no time; they were insensible to everything – 'it is a delirium of joy, a very fury of delight!'

In the centre the *Queen Charlotte*, way ahead of all but the *Brunswick* on her starboard quarter, closed the stern of the *Montagne* with Howe himself conning. The ship following the French admiral, the *Jacobin*, had seen his intention and made sail to close the gap Howe was steering for; at the same time the *Montagne* backed her sails so that the *Jacobin*, closing fast, had to sheer off to leeward where she took up the position Howe was making for very close on the lee quarter of the flagship. Undeterred, Howe stood on, through the fire of the Jacobin and her next astern. The *Charlotte*'s Master growled approvingly, 'That's right, my Lord, the *Charlotte* will make room for herself!'

As they swept across the *Montagne*'s stern and the foremost larboard guns opened a raking fire through Villaret's richly carved galleries, Howe ordered the helm to starboard. The Master called out that it would take them aboard the *Jacobin*. 'What is that to you, sir?' Howe snapped. 'Starboard!' the Master repeated, and muttered, 'Damn my eyes if I care if *you* don't!'

'That's a fine fellow,' Howe remarked to his First Captain.

The *Jacobin*, seeing the three-decker bearing down straight upon her, paid off to leeward and the *Queen Charlotte* passed through the

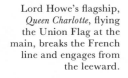

Lord Howe's flagship, *Queen Charlotte*, flying the Union Flag at the main, breaks the French line and engages from the leeward.

narrow gap she left, giving her her starboard guns as she did so. Howe was carrying such a press of sail that his lower ports were almost level with the sea, which poured through green and swept the deck like a tide. As Howe luffed up a-lee of the *Montagne*, and so close he nearly scraped her quarter, his fore topmast, whose rigging had been shot away during the approach, fell; at the same time the leech (side) of the main topsail was split by a ball from the *Jacobin* and the sail ceased to be of any use as the flagship hauled to the wind. But her momentum carried her up abreast of the *Montagne* and her larboard guns, which had already opened a breech in the French stern 'large enough to row the admiral's barge through', poured a murderous fire into her hull, the timbers of which were pierced no less than 230 times in a short space, and some three hundred of her men were killed or wounded.

Astern of these three, Captain Harvey of the *Brunswick* had been unable to cut through as the French ships following the *Jacobin* had made sail to close the line. But, like Howe, he held on, forcing the second, the *Vengeur du Peuple*, to bear up, but so late that her fore shrouds and chains hooked his starboard anchor; the two ships locked and swung together yardarm to yardarm, and there began the most desperate close duel. Where the ships' hull timbers ground together in the swell it was impossible to raise the port lids and the crews fired their pieces without running them out through closed port lids straight into the enemy decks less than a cannon's length away, dousing the fires started with buckets of water. Soon the British guns' crews were alternately elevating and depressing their pieces to extreme angles, tearing up through the French deck beams with some shots, down through the bottom timbers with the reload.

Just astern, the *Valiant* went through the gap created as the *Vengeur* closed for the *Brunswick*, and shortly afterwards the three-decker *Queen*, ahead of most of the rear division, passed through easily when her opponent bore away downwind. During the approach the *Queen* suffered severely in masts and rigging, but she was able to round up and engage the next ahead from two hundred yards to leeward, the distance closing to pistol shot as the French-man tried to escape past her. The *Royal George*, four ships from the rear, went through at about the same time.

These seven were the only ones to follow Howe's signal '34', although later on the *Glory*, at the extreme eastern end of the line, got to leeward around the French rear. By this time the French line was in such confusion with many of those not shrouded in the smoke of close mêlées retiring downwind, that the British captains 31

The French flagship, *Montagne*, looking remarkably undamaged, but with her stern timbers and hull holed and riven with shot from the *Queen Charlotte*, forges ahead towards the mêlée at the head of the line.

who had not kept up with the leaders did not attempt to get to leeward – some because they could not without passing through their own consorts' fire, or firing into them, others because they thought Howe's signal '34' permissive, or lacked resolution. So they rounded into the wind in irregular order wherever they could find an enemy to engage in the traditional way from two hundred yards or so to windward, or sailed up what had been the French line to find an opponent from the smoke. One of these was the *Gibraltar* whose position had been immediately to larboard of the *Queen Charlotte*. Her captain had so little idea of the meaning of Howe's signals that he made no attempt to follow through the line, but luffed up some distance off and fired into the mêlée about the French Commander-in-Chief. Before long he was firing into the *Charlotte* herself as the *Montagne*, her hull riven and her guns' crews decimated but with rigging and sails little hurt, forged ahead of the British flagship, which had lost her main topmast soon after the fore topmast and could not keep up. The captain of the British flagship fell to the *Gibraltar*'s fire.

32   At about the same time, a short distance ahead, Rear-Admiral

Bowyer of the *Barfleur* had a leg taken from under him by a ball; Captain Collingwood caught him as he fell. The *Barfleur* was one of those which had been unable to get up to the enemy line without passing through the fire of the British ships to larboard, but Collingwood had taken her 'very near indeed, and then began such a fire as would have done you good to have heard'. Three ships ahead of him, the fiercest mêlée of the day was taking place around the *Defence* and *Marlborough*. Both of these had engaged their opponents from close to leeward at the start, disabled them in a short time by cutting all their rigging and masts close to the deck with the tremendous volume of their shot, silenced their guns and started numerous fires which the survivors were attempting to extinguish. Meanwhile other French ships had worn around and fallen on them, attempting to board; the *Marlborough* had dismasted her second opponent and was attempting to back clear of the two wrecks when a third enemy, the French flagship, *Montagne*, came across her stern, backed the main topsail to hold herself there and commenced a terrible raking fire which completed the destruction of the British vessel's rigging and brought all three

The British *Defence*, first ship to break the line, now dismasted and surrounded by the enemy, still keeps firing: 'The guns were so heated that when we fired they nearly kicked the upper deck beams ...'.

33

The epic contest between the *Brunswick* (centre) and *Vengeur du Peuple*; with the ships locked together the guns' crews fired their pieces, without running them out, through closed gun ports straight into the enemy decks.

masts crashing over the side. The captain of the *Marlborough* was wounded at the same time and taken below; his first lieutenant took over command and, determined not to yield, had a Union Jack bent to the spritsail yard and a St George's ensign nailed to the stump of the foremast until he found that the *Gibraltar* and *Culloden*, which had both sailed up from the mêlée around the *Queen Charlotte*, still to windward, mistook this for the French ensign and fired into his wallowing hulk.

The *Defence* close by had lost her main and mizen masts; her exhausted guns' crews, having silenced her first opponent, were

keeping up a constant fire into fresh enemy ships coming from the rear and passing to leeward. The conditions on her lower deck especially were nightmarish: water was surging feet deep from side to side, a gun had broken loose and was careering about as the ship rolled and the whole space

was at times so completely filled with smoke that we could scarcely distinguish each other and the guns were so heated that when we fired they nearly kicked the upper deck beams. The metal became so hot that, fearing some accident, we reduced the quantity of powder, allowing also more time to elapse between the loading and the firing of them.   35

By eleven o'clock all semblance of the original lines had dissolved; clusters of hulks with stumps of masts and wreckage hanging overside wallowed about the seven British which had broken through to leeward at the start and were almost equally damaged. Most of the French ships were silent and many had struck their colours in surrender; those which had not been caught and held to close action in this way had succeeded in retiring downwind where Villaret had rallied them and formed another line some three miles to leeward of the mêlée. Meanwhile those British ships which had opened from the windward berth and were consequently not so damaged still sailed towards what had been the head of the French line, picking opponents where they could find them from the

Lord Howe on the quarterdeck of the *Queen Charlotte* with a panorama of the battle behind; a heroic rendering of the death of his Flag Captain.

smoke. One of these was the *Ramillies*, whose captain, Henry Harvey, was the brother of the captain of the *Brunswick*, still locked in her epic struggle with the *Vengeur*. Harvey took the *Ramillies* down across the *Vengeur*'s lee quarter and opened a raking fire into her hull which destroyed her completely, opening so many more holes low down that she filled and sank a few hours later. His brother was not on deck to see it; wounded three times, he had gone below to have his arm amputated; he survived for just one month.

Towards 11.30 the guns were falling silent, and by midday the smoke had cleared to reveal nine French and two British ships totally dismasted, and several others with only one mast standing, all scattered over some four miles. Howe was attempting to collect his fleet and form line as best he could to leeward of the French hulks to secure them from rescue attempts by Villaret. His frigates, whose battle station had been on the disengaged side of the line, were in amongst them, passing cables to those ships which needed a tow and sending boarding parties to the enemy hulks which had not been taken in possession. Meanwhile Villaret's new line to leeward was threatening to cut off the *Queen*, which had lost her mainmast, and the *Defence* and *Marlborough*, which were unmanageable and had drifted down towards them. Villaret's frigates were towing off their own disabled ships which they could reach, while other French hulks, which had not yet been boarded, had set spritsails under their bows and were also drifting off downwind to rejoin their fleet. A few British line ships, which had either failed to take in Howe's signal to form line of battle ahead and astern of the flagship as most convenient, or had chosen to disregard it, were attempting to cut off the escaping French, at least one of which had actually struck her colours before seizing the opportunity to make off. It was a scene of vast confusion.

By this time Howe was totally exhausted: it was the fifth day of contact with the enemy, the third day of constant manoeuvring, and the *Queen Charlotte* had been in close action twice – on this occasion with three ships as, having lost the *Montagne* in the smoke, she had come up to leeward of her next ahead, the *Juste*, and reduced her to a dismasted wreck. Now his years told. As a younger man he might have made the signal for a general chase and borne down again on the enemy, both to secure the escaping French hulks and to drive Villaret's new-formed line into confusion. But it is not certain that he would have done so – or made any other attacking move. He was not sure of all his captains, particularly those with the least damaged ships who should have been able to do most in a chase action, for they were the very ones who had

The *Royal George* and *Marlborough*, dismasted and unmanageable after the battle.

failed him that morning, and he felt this strongly. Besides, the *Queen Charlotte* was so damaged aloft that she could only sail down-wind and many of the other ships which still retained their masts were little better.

In any case, so weary he could scarcely stand, he left the decisions to Sir Roger Curtis, his First Captain. Curtis, seeing Villaret's ships formed apparently in good order and, as he thought, threatening to turn the tables on the separated British ships, recalled all those that were chasing lest they were cut off too, and after sailing down in some sort of line to rescue the isolated *Queen*, held the fleet together to meet any counter-attack. As a result five of the severely mauled French escaped back to their own lines as Howe, tottering on legs that would no longer support him against the roll of the ship, was helped by several officers and midshipmen down to his quarters. 'Why, you hold me as if I were a child,' he said as they got him into his cot.

Afterwards there was criticism of Curtis for his caution, then and the following day when the British fleet allowed Villaret to retire from the scene without pursuing. But at the time probably most of the captains were well content with as shattering a victory as had ever been achieved between numerically equal fleets. They retained six of the wrecked French as prizes, while the *Vengeur du Peuple*, which had put up a truly heroic defence for longer than any other, capsized and sank in the early evening, taking over a hundred of her surviving crew with her. Seven out of twenty-six was a brilliant result, even if it might have been twelve. Collingwood expressed most officers' feelings when he wrote, 'We who were seamen were well acquainted with the great professional abilities of Lord Howe; but he has outdone all opinion that could be formed. The proceedings of the 1st of June were like magic, and could only be effected by skill like his.' As for the men of the *Queen Charlotte*, a deputation approached the ship's Master to ask if they might congratulate Howe and thank him for leading them 'so gloriously into battle'. Howe received them on the quarterdeck, visibly affected by the gesture, and with faltering voice and eyes glistening with tears replied, 'No – no – I thank *you*. It is *you*, my brave lads – it is you, not I that have conquered.'

Because of the failure to harass or pursue Villaret, and because Howe then sailed for England instead of continuing to seek the convoy, the series of actions culminating in 'The Glorious First of June', in spite of being a triumphant victory, must be viewed as a strategic failure of enormous magnitude. The American convoy with its rich supplies of grain reached Brest safely on 17 June – one day after Villaret himself. Nevertheless the main battle was a significant tactical breakthrough which inaugurated a new and uniquely triumphant era of naval warfare. No longer could the French expect to escape close action in line of battle by bearing away downwind; Villaret's undoubted skill in controlling his fleet only emphasised the point. British tactics and signals had caught up with gunnery superiority – which in this case had claimed 3,500 enemy against only 1,100 British killed and wounded. It merely remained to capitalise on this. As one officer present at the battle remarked, 'the First of June was the *first* general action fought in

the course of the war ... had it been the *last* not one of the French
ships would have been allowed to return to port'.

As always at the beginning of a war the moral effects of victory
were as important as material results. With little to show from their
army in Europe, disillusioned with their continental allies, the
British people could take heart as of old from the exploits of their
unconquerable Navy. The toast was 'May the French ever know
Howe to be master of the sea!'

The British fleet
(*Queen Charlotte* left
foreground) brings six
dismasted prizes under
jury rig into Spithead
after the battle.

Chapter 2

St Vincent

In the Mediterranean the British squadron under Lord Hood was in an equally commanding position. At one time the previous summer, almost the whole of the powerful French fleet in Toulon had fallen into their hands when that naval arsenal had risen against the Revolution. Hood had lacked sufficient troops to hold the port for long against a Jacobin assault from inland, but when forced to leave in December he had taken three French sail of the line with him and burned another nine. A Spanish party supposedly helping the British to destroy the ships had been deliberately inefficient as their commander had no desire to tilt the balance of naval power decisively in Britain's favour by wiping out the entire French Mediterranean fleet! Consequently the Jacobins entering Toulon regained fourteen of the line for the Republic. But with inexperienced commanders and disaffected or mutinous crews they were of little use. Hood had no difficulty in chasing them back to harbour when they ventured to sea, meanwhile enforcing a strict commercial blockade of the French Mediterranean coast, and supporting British troop landings to seize and hold the island of Corsica as a secure base and provisioning centre for the fleet. Foremost in the Corsican adventure was Captain Horatio Nelson, in command of the 64-gun *Agamemnon*. As yet unknown outside the service and most remarkable within it for a burning, impetuous, even desperate desire for personal glory, his extraordinary enthusiasm and flair had been marked by all those he had served under. Lord Hood was no exception. They had first met some twelve years earlier towards the end of the American War of Independence when Nelson had been a frigate captain; he had obtained his promotion to this 'Post' rank three years before by a mixture of early patronage, good fortune, keenness and ability while still under the statutory age of twenty-one. His slight figure, rather less than five feet six inches in height, undistinguished features, lank hair, old-fashioned uniform and absurdly youthful appearance, 'the merest boy of a captain', had given no hint of his unusual qualities. But when he spoke his features lit and his eager intelligence broke through. One witness to the meeting wrote, 'there was something irresistible pleasing in his address and conversation; and an enthusiasm when speaking on professional subjects that showed he was no common being'. Hood was impressed and remained so despite a disastrously hasty assault on a French-held island in the Bahamas which the young captain attempted on his own initiative with sailors and Marines from three small ships in company. This was not Nelson's first abortive shore attack.

Nelson and British soldiers and sailors from *Captain* board the Spanish *San Nicolas*.

43

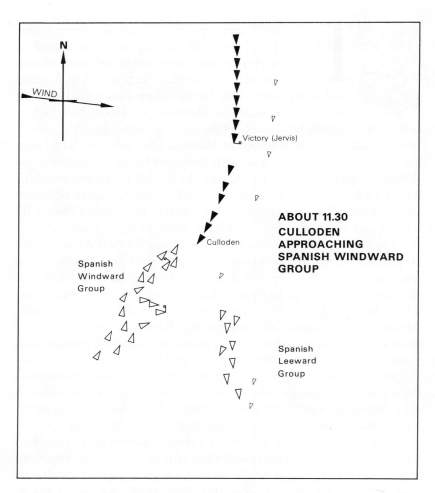

N

WIND

Victory (Jervis)

**ABOUT 11.30
CULLODEN
APPROACHING
SPANISH WINDWARD
GROUP**

Culloden

Spanish
Windward
Group

Spanish
Leeward
Group

Map 2
The turning point of
Battle of St Vincent.

Before meeting Hood he had escorted a force of soldiers to the San
Juan river for an assault across Spanish Nicaragua; not content
with assuring their safe arrival, he had led the assault boats up
river and, before going down with yellow fever, had taken such an
active part in the operations against Fort San Juan that the commanding officer of the troops thought 'there was scarcely a gun
fired but was pointed by him'.

That expedition was a costly disaster, and the American war
had ended without allowing Nelson the chance of renown he
craved. During the peace before the Revolutionary War when so
many officers wiled away their time on half pay, Lord Hood's
interest secured him command of another frigate in which he sailed
for the West Indies. Here he found the Commander-in-Chief on

44

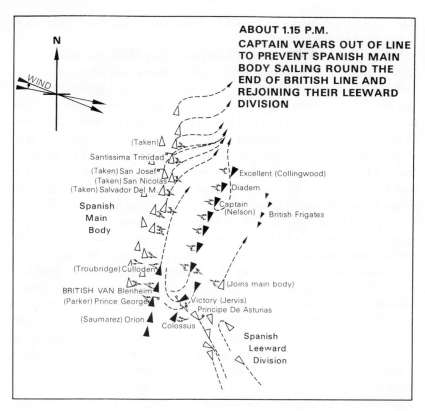

ABOUT 1.15 P.M.

CAPTAIN WEARS OUT OF LINE
TO PREVENT SPANISH MAIN
BODY SAILING ROUND THE
END OF BRITISH LINE AND
REJOINING THEIR LEEWARD
DIVISION

N

WIND

(Taken)
Santissima Trinidad
(Taken) San Josef
(Taken) San Nicolas
(Taken) Salvador Del M.

Excellent (Collingwood)
Diadem
Captain
(Nelson)
British Frigates

Spanish
Main
Body

(Troubridge) Culloden
BRITISH VAN Blenheim
(Parker) Prince George
(Saumarez) Orion
Colossus

(Joins main body)

Victory (Jervis)
Principe De Asturias

Spanish
Leeward
Division

Map 3
Opening of the Battle
of St Vincent, 14
February 1797.

the station and all about him 'great ninnies', and moreover con-
niving with the islands' merchants in breach of the Navigation
Laws of England by trading with Americans, formerly colonial
subjects of the King, but as a result of the late war *foreigners*; the
Navigation Laws placed restrictions on trade with foreigners.
Although his Commander-in-Chief turned a blind eye to wholesale disregard of these laws which interfered with long-established
trades, Nelson in defiance of his orders, turned back every American
vessel he came across, raising a storm of anger and litigation from
merchants and shipowners and threats of court martial from his
Commander-in-Chief. Certain of rectitude in upholding his
country's laws contrary to orders – a decision which would have
posed great problems for an officer less single-minded and confident, or less artless than Nelson – he maintained his stand and
persuaded the Admiralty to pay for his defence against the American shipowners. He was supported by other captains on the station,
notably his great friend, Cuthbert Collingwood; this did not help
his popularity, and he returned home two years later with a name 45

that was secure in the islands for many years to come – although not as he had wished it.

While in the West Indies he married; after returning to England he was placed on half pay, and made a home with his wife at his father's vicarage at Burnham Thorpe in Norfolk, attempting for the next five years to channel his ardent nature into the slow round of country life. He was rescued by the outbreak of the Revolutionary War. Appointed to command the 64-gun *Agamemnon*, his first 'line' ship – although 64's were the weakest type considered fit to lie in lines of battle which were formed almost exclusively of 74's with a few heavier rates for flagships and their 'seconds' – he poured everything into her. His prime gift had always been the affection he inspired in all who served with him; his nature was so open, his spirit so vehement and contained in such a frail-looking vessel, his enthusiasm was so infectious, his humanity and his interest in whomever he addressed from the admiral to the powder monkey were all so evident and natural it was impossible not to respond. Added to this power of inspiration, and love is not too strong a term, he had a mind which grasped the essentials of situations with speed and precision, hence reacted while others were often thinking – above all an extraordinary confidence in his own conclusions which allowed him to dispense with compromise and take the most outrageous initiatives. And he was physically fearless – or appeared so. While his unconcealed hunger for the limelight and the unnatural zest with which he chased it appeared ridiculous, even dangerous to many steady good officers, to those who knew him best, to his ships' companies and to successive commanders-

The 64-gun *Agamemnon*, commanded by Nelson, manoeuvres across the stern of the 80-gun *Ca Ira*, raking and reducing her to a wreck.

in-chief he was irresistible. This was true of Hood; in the Mediterranean he soon recognised him as one of his ablest captains for any independent mission. It was equally true of the Agamemnons; how could it be otherwise when he had such unaffected pride in *them*? 'My seamen are now what British seamen ought to be ... almost invincible. They really mind shot no more than peas,' and 'I always was of opinion that one Englishman was equal to three Frenchmen.' As for the ship herself, she was 'without exception the finest 64 in the service'.

With such a captain it was not surprising that the Agamemnons found themselves at the centre of action in the Mediterranean, laying siege to the town of Bastia in Corsica after Nelson had persuaded Hood that the soldiers 'go too slow', soon marching in to the town victorious, hauling ships' cannon over almost impassable mountainous country to assault the Corsican port of Calvi from inland – where Nelson received a scattering of sand and stones from a shot which damaged his right eye permanently – in 1795 after a Corsican base had been secured and Hood had gone home on leave, in the van during two partial engagements with the Toulon fleet, in the first reducing the 80-gun *Ca Ira* to a wreck so that she and one other which had taken her in tow had to strike the following morning, in the second helping to batter a 74 which eventually caught fire and blew up. Both these actions reinforced Nelson in the belief – inspired by one of his first captains – that it was only necessary to lay a Frenchman close to beat him. In both he had scented sure fleet victory and had gone aboard the flagship to implore his new Commander-in-Chief to chase and settle the business; on both occasions the admiral's caution prevented what – to judge by the deplorable state of the French ships and crews – should have resulted in annihilation of the Toulon fleet. To his wife, Nelson wrote:

> I wish to be an Admiral and in command of the English fleet; I should very soon either do much or be ruined. My disposition cannot bear tame or slow measures. Sure I am, had I commanded our Fleet on the 14th, that either the whole French fleet would have graced my triumph, or I should have been in a confounded scrape.

After these missed opportunities Nelson was sent in command of a detached squadron to blockade the Gulf of Genoa and support Austrian armies resisting a French assault into the north Italian territories of the Habsburg Empire. While on this service his too languid Commander-in-Chief was replaced by Admiral Sir John Jervis – a man of very different mettle which matched his own.

It was none too soon. By this time the war on land had taken a

47

disastrous turn for the coalition of monarchies against France. The early days when victory had seemed almost too easy against the divided and chaotically disordered Republic had been frittered away with too many diversions of effort, too many national interests taking precedence, too many failures in allied co-operation. The Republic had been given time. During that time the central administration had been strengthened by Robespierre with terrifying single-mindedness, the citizen army had been born, infused with a sense of mission to liberate all peoples oppressed by monarchy. In the autumn of 1794 one of these armies, helped by a fatal lack of co-ordination between the allies, had swept up through Flanders to the Scheldt. In January 1795 they had entered Amsterdam; that spring the Prince of Orange fled, Holland became the Batavian Republic allied to France, the greater part of her fleet, surprised while still ice-bound in the Texel, counted as one with the French fleets. Meanwhile Prussia dropped out of the alliance, giving to the French all her territories west of the Rhine; in April the British army sailed for home from Bremen.

That summer Spain made her peace with the Republic, whose northern army shortly swept across the Rhine to 'liberate' then plunder the smaller German states. In 1796 it was Austria's turn. The dangerously ambitious General Bonaparte was given his head to cross the Alps and strike at the rich Austrian territories in the valley of the Po. Against great natural and numerical odds his campaign became a triumph. In the autumn of 1796 Spain turned right around and threw in her lot with this new and explosively powerful France; with the prospect of her numerous sail of the line joined to the French fleet in Toulon, with the north Italian coastline and its plentiful supplies barred to British ships by Bonaparte's successes, with the Corsicans rising against occupation and the British garrison too small to deal with the threat effectively, the British government decided to evacuate the Mediterranean. The fleet was ordered to Gibraltar and from there at the end of the year to Lisbon, where it would be better placed to concentrate with the home fleets at the western end of the Channel in the event of a Spanish fleet sailing north to join the French in Brest. The government viewed the possibility seriously; they had intelligence of an army being assembled at Brest for the invasion of Ireland.

Preparations for this attempt had been going forward since early autumn. Seventeen sail of the line, numerous frigates and transports with more than twenty thousand soldiers and their horses, stores and the military supply train had been assembled under the enthusiastic direction of General Lazare Hoche. Hoche had been longing to strike at the British on their own soil for years; now the conditions were right: Ireland was alive with discontent and the seductive doctrines of Liberty and 'Natural Rights' on which the French Republic had been launched. Leading Irish Republicans had convinced themselves – and Hoche – that it only needed a French army to land and the country would rise against the British. Once Ireland had been liberated, it was but a step to the home country itself, while the possession of Irish harbours would enable French and Spanish squadrons to sever all British trade routes from the Atlantic. The chief obstacles to the attempt were of course the British Channel Fleet with its advanced squadron of frigates hovering arrogantly off the very mouth of the Iroise exit to the Atlantic, and the lamentable state of the French ships themselves. Starved of supplies by the government's concentration on the

Sir Edward Pellew, the most celebrated frigate captain of his day.

army, together with the British disruption of the coastal trade in timber and other essentials, and with the problems created by the break-up of the old officer corps still unsolved, the performance of the Brest fleet over the two years since the 'First of June' had been humiliating. Villaret felt it so deeply and was so pessimistic about the expedition's chances that he had been replaced; the new Commander-in-Chief was Vice-Admiral Morard de Galles, whose own recent experiences of crews refusing duty in the face of a weaker enemy squadron could not have made him much more optimistic.

Sir Edward Pellew
manoeuvres the
frigate *Indefatigable* into
a position of advantage
off the bows of the 74-
gun ship of the line
Droits de l'homme.

But Hoche's enthusiasm prevailed. Without waiting for Spanish reinforcements the expedition weighed on a fair easterly wind at twilight in the evening of 16 December 1796. De Galles had decided to dodge the British observation squadron off the Iroise Channel by taking an alternative exit route south-south-westerly into the Bay of Biscay. But as the leading ships got under way the wind veered southerly, gusting, and he signalled them to leave by the usual westerly route into the Atlantic. In the darkness his signals were not taken in, while those made by gun were confused by distress signals from a 74 which had impaled herself on the rocks of the southern passage. To add to the disorder which ensued, the commander of the British squadron of observation, Sir Edward Pellew, the most celebrated frigate captain of the day, sailed in amongst the mêlée firing off cannon and rockets and lighting blue flares at random – enjoying himself hugely while providing an incomprehensible display of pyrotechnic signals.

As a result of these alarms the expedition became separated into detachments which took their own courses into the Atlantic out of touch with the others. Meanwhile de Galles himself, his Chief of Staff, Bruix, and General Hoche, who had all embarked in the fast frigate, *Fraternité*, had become separated from everyone. Fortunately for them no British squadrons were at hand to take advantage of the position; Pellew had sent all his frigates off with news of the French movement but the blockading squadron had been blown from its station and the main body of the Channel Fleet was lying in Portsmouth – dangerous lapses in the face of such obvious invasion preparations. Most of the separated groups of French ships steered south-westerly into the Atlantic, making Pellew think they were destined for Portugal, then drove north in easterly gales without sighting any British ships, and after meeting each other near the appointed rendezvous, they sailed into Bantry Bay at the southern tip of Ireland on 22 December. One of the exceptions was the *Fraternité* with the chief commanders aboard. In searching for her fleet she had the misfortune to meet a British ship of the line and was chased far to the westward. The easterly gales which continued with increased violence not only prevented her from making back to the rendezvous, they made it almost impossible for the unskilled crews of the fleet now in Bantry Bay to work their ships up the north-easterly trend of the bay towards the chosen landing places for the troops; those ships at anchor dragged, several were forced out to sea and two frigates were driven aground. With bitterly cold weather and snow driving in with the storm, over-crowded ships, the men wet and daily growing more miserable at the continued foul winds, above all with food beginning to run low and without the inspiration of Hoche, the second-in-command abandoned the enterprise on 25 December and sailed for home.

The invasion fleet left, as they had started, in separated groups with stragglers. One of the last of these was the 74-gun *Droits de l'homme* with a battalion of troops aboard in addition to her sailors. The following month, as she was nearing home in a rising south-westerly gale, she had the misfortune to fall in with Sir Edward

Pellew in the *Indefatigable*, back on station with another frigate, *Amazon*, in company; hardly had she sighted the British ships than a sudden gust carried away both her fore and main topmasts. This was too much for Pellew. Although frigates were no match for ships of the line and seldom engaged them, a damaged and over-crowded ship labouring in high seas which would make it difficult for her to use the lower guns, extraordinarily difficult to hull such a low target as a frigate, was fair game. He chased as she ran off downwind, and, catching her just as the winter darkness closed, opened the engagement with a raking broadside into her stern. The French captain manoeuvred to bring his own broadside to bear and Pellew shot ahead and took up a position across his bows to rake again. So the contest continued downwind with the

The *Indefatigable*, now joined by the frigate *Amazon*, reduces the *Droits de l'homme* to a wreck: note the battleship's lower gun ports are closed due to heavy weather.

Amazon steering for the gun flashes and, reaching the scene about an hour later, adding her fire to the *Indefatigable*'s. With only brief intervals to repair damages and splice the rigging the two British frigates hung either side of the 74's bows throughout the night as the wind and sea rose, and, evading the French captain's attempts to run them aboard, poured their fire into his crowded hull, bringing down his mizen mast and killing or wounding more than 250 men. The French replied whenever they could get their guns to bear, but although they expended all their round shot and had to continue with shells, most went into the sea or overhead through the rigging, and the total British casualties were only thirty-seven.

The critical point of the action came at 4.30 in the morning when the guns' crews were dropping from exhaustion; a sudden shaft of moonlight illumined land and lines of breakers before it only a mile and a half ahead – downwind. At once the fight was forgotten. Pellew signalled the *Amazon* that she was standing in to danger and immediately put his ship about. It was the first of a long series of tacks with which he eventually clawed her out of

The end of a unique encounter; *Droits de l'homme* takes the ground as Pellew, beating off the lee shore, fires rockets to warn the *Amazon* of the danger.

what proved to be the south side of a bay fringed with lines of rocks extending seawards; it was Audierne Bay south of Brest. The *Amazon* failed to escape. She had lost her mizen in the fight and, unable to tack, tried to wear around, but she was too close to the land and grounded. Nearly all her crew escaped later on extemporised rafts. The *Droits de l'homme* had even less chance than the *Amazon*; she drove ashore broadside on, heeled over and in the ensuing scramble to escape hundreds more lost their lives.

Pellew's feat, never surpassed by a frigate captain, of driving a ship of the line to her destruction, was a fitting end to an expedition he had helped on its way with such panache. But both sides had come badly out of the larger affair, the British Admiralty and the Channel Fleet commanded by Lord Bridport perhaps worst of all; they claimed to rule the seas, yet they had allowed an armada of ships carrying a military expedition one and a half times larger than the combined garrisons in Ireland an unmolested passage in the most sensitive area to and from their chosen landing place, and had only been saved from the consequences by the chances of the weather and the irresolution of the second-in-command. The expedition was now back at its base, largely intact; the possibilities of Spanish reinforcements and a second attempt were infinitely dangerous.

The Commander-in-Chief of the former Mediterranean Fleet marking the Spanish force preparing to sail for Brest measured up to the scale of the challenge. John Jervis' character had been forged in adversity. Without influential connections, without family support, as a midshipman he had been so hard pressed for money that he had been forced to leave the gunroom mess and find a berth wherever he could on deck, make and mend his own clothes, seek companionship wherever he could find it among those stalwart petty and warrant officers who formed the backbone of the service, make up for what he missed in youthful antics by work and study. He had emerged from the ordeal with formidable inner reserves of discipline and self-reliance, and immense professional competence which soon brought him advancement. He insisted on his own high standards in his fleet; uncompromising in discipline – but scrupulously fair – he had fashioned it by constant gun drill and work at sea into an extension of his own single-minded devotion to the service. 'At home they know not what this fleet is capable of performing,' Nelson wrote to his wife, 'anything and everything   55

and with a Commander-in-Chief fit to lead them to Glory.'

The admiration was mutual. Aboard his flagship, *Victory*, Jervis, who had a penetrating eye for a man's strengths and weaknesses, was writing of Nelson as 'the best and fittest fellow in the world; yet his zeal does now and then (not often) outrun his discretion'.

In early 1797 Nelson was on detached service again; he had transferred to the fast frigate *Minerve*, and with the frigate *Blanche* in company was in the Mediterranean completing the evacuation of Corsica and a garrison at Elba – at the same time gathering intelligence of Spanish fleet preparations. On the way from Gibraltar he had fallen in with two Spanish frigates and, being Nelson, had chased and fought a spirited night action resulting in the capture of both. However, no sooner had a prize crew got aboard the *Minerve*'s opponent, the 40-gun *Santa Sabina*, than three other

56

Spanish men-of-war including one of the line loomed up and the *Minerve* and *Blanche* had to run for it, leaving the *Sabina* and her prize crew to be recaptured – a turn which mortified Nelson, although Jervis attempted to console him with a letter expressing admiration at his 'glorious achievement, and dignified retreat from the line of battle ship which deprived you of your well-earned trophy'.

On the return voyage Nelson, stretching into all the enemy ports, found that the Spanish fleet had sailed; calling at Gibraltar he learned that they had passed westerly through the Straits four days previously. He also learned that Lieutenant Hardy and other members of the captured prize crew from the *Sabina* were aboard a small detachment of the fleet which had been left at anchor near by in the bay. As he had the *Sabina*'s captain aboard the *Minerve* he arranged an exchange of prisoners, then set sail to carry the news to Jervis. As he weighed, two of the Spanish sail of the line in the Bay were seen to be under way steering to cut him off and, the headmost soon showing herself a good sailer, another and hopelessly unequal engagement seemed likely. Nelson, pacing the quarterdeck with the animation he always displayed at the prospect of action, looked up at his broad pennant, confiding to one of the officers he had taken from Elba, 'Before the Dons get hold of that bit of bunting I'll have a struggle with them. Sooner than give up the frigate, I'll run her ashore!' Shortly afterwards, as the studding sails were being set, one of the sailors fell overboard; the jolly boat was run down to the water and with the recently exchanged Lieutenant Hardy in the sternsheets, pointed astern and pulled smartly back along the wake to where the man had disappeared. After a vain search, during which the boat dropped a long way behind the *Minerve*, still running from the leading Spaniard, now almost within gunshot, they attempted to pull back. On board the frigate their chances of making it before the Spaniard caught up looked slim – whereupon Nelson made one of his rapid, highly individual judgements. 'By God, I'll not lose Hardy!' he exclaimed, and ordered the mizen topsail backed.

The *Minerve*'s way was checked, the jolly boat's crew responded with extra heart, and were soon aboard; the Spaniard, meanwhile, apparently thinking the British meant to fight it out, shortened sail and waited for her consort to come up to support. Afterwards the *Minerve*'s studding sails were set and she walked away, losing both pursuers after dark. The respite was not for long. It was a foggy night, and they soon found they had strayed into the middle of a fleet and were sailing between two strange ships of the line, both within hail, with many more around them on all hands; from their signals it was evident they were not British. Nelson concluded that he had either chanced on the Spanish grand fleet or on a Spanish West Indian convoy – 'something of a scrape, although I believe with address we may extricate ourselves'. This they managed in the fog, and, certain by the following morning from the course the ships steered that they had indeed been the Spanish fleet under Admiral Joséf de Cordova, Nelson made all sail to Jervis' fleet, reaching it at the rendezvous off Cape St Vincent that afternoon, 13 February 1797.

Jervis already had reports of the Spanish movement out of the Mediterranean and was waiting for them off this south-westerly tip of the Iberian peninsula which they must round if their destination were to the north. Nelson's news confirmed his intelligence. Just as important was the information which Lieutenant Hardy and his companions were able to provide from their observations of the Spanish ships while in captivity. Hopelessly short of trained men, even Cordova's flagships had no more than sixty to eighty sailors aboard; for the rest the crews were made up with pressed landsmen who had never been to sea and levies of equally raw soldiers; with a shortage of supplies of all kinds neither ships nor men were in any way ready to fight. This also agreed with previous reports, and despite a prohibitive inferiority in numbers – fifteen of the line against twenty-seven or more reported under Cordova – Jervis was confirmed in his decision to force a fight. Soon after four o'clock that afternoon numeral flags '53' – 'Prepare for Battle' – fluttered from the *Victory*'s halyards. As Nelson left the flagship to go aboard the 74-gun *Captain*, to which Jervis had transferred him, ships' carpenters attacked partitions of the officers' quarters to leave a clean run from bows to stern windows, sailors stowed furniture and personal belongings below, loosed the great guns and ran them out, provided each with its instruments and round shot, wads and half-casks for brine and matches; sandbags were hoisted and emptied in heaps on deck, swept across the planks; above, chain slings were rove as additional supports for the yards; below in the hazy lantern-light on the orlop deck, surgeons looked over their chests of instruments and medications as carpenters knocked up platforms for the wounded and spread clean canvas. At an early dinner aboard the flagship that evening the toast was 'Victory over the Dons in the battle from which they cannot escape tomorrow!'

That night enemy signal guns were heard from the southward, becoming more distinct towards dawn on the 14th – St Valentine's day. Jervis was up at first light. He had already received a report from a Portuguese frigate which had chanced upon them in the small hours that the Spaniards were fifteen miles to windward. He paced the deck more than usually silent, his jaw thrust forward low over thick, hunched shoulders, his eyes hard and very blue as he peered into a morning haze which shut out all but the nearest ships. The fleet was formed in two divisions, steering south-easterly under easy sail to a wind from the south-west. He was pleased with the admirably close order that had been maintained during the night; it was only by such tight concentration that he could hope to defeat an enemy twice his force. He voiced his appreciation to the officers near by, adding: 'A victory is very essential to England at this moment.'

As the haze began to lift soon after six o'clock the first reports of strange sail began to come in from the frigates stationed to windward. Jervis had the reefs shaken out of his topsails and set his topgallants as the wind, fortunately veering towards the west, allowed

Gun deck of the *Victory*; note rammers and sponges above guns.

59

him to steer an ever more southerly course. By 6.30 some of the enemy topsails and t'gallants could be seen from the *Victory*. An hour later, with more sail visible, now stretching from the south-south-west to the south-south-easterly horizon although in no discernible order, Jervis signalled his most weatherly sloop, the *Bonne Citoyenne*, to go ahead and reconnoitre.

Before she could report it began to appear as if the enemy must be in two separated groups, the most easterly or leeward of which was on the same starboard tack as the British fleet and running; Jervis ordered his Rear-Admiral's flagship, the three-decker *Prince George*, together with one other three-decker, and the 74-gun *Culloden*, captain Thomas Troubridge – whom Jervis considered the best officer in the service – to chase. They set main courses, staysails and drivers and with royals spread above the t'gallants drove towards the leeward straggle of ships. Shortly afterwards Jervis ordered two more 74's to join them, and when the *Orion*, captain Sir James Saumarez, also pressed on sail, he signalled his approval. Confirmation that the enemy was in two groups soon came from the frigate *Minerve*, reporting one to be twenty strong, the other eight; this was followed by signals intimating increasing numbers. Finally the *Bonne Citoyenne* reported that twenty-seven of the enemy were ships of the line. When this was reported and the captain of the fleet commented on the great disparity in force, Jervis cut him short, 'Enough, sir! No more of that. If there are fifty sail I will go through them!'

This so delighted Captain Hallowell, a passenger aboard the *Victory*, and now pacing the deck with the Admiral, that he forgot himself and clapped his hand on Jervis' back. 'That's right, Sir John – that's right! By God, we shall give them a damned good licking!'

By now it was apparent that although the enemy group to leeward was on the starboard tack, running southerly, the main body of the enemy to windward was heading north on the larboard tack; they had shortened sail and several had brought to, evidently forming line of battle. To prevent them from bearing down and joining their separated ships, Jervis steered for the gap between the groups, again fortunate in a shift of wind to west by north, which allowed him a south-south-westerly course; he signalled the fleet to form line of battle ahead and astern as most convenient. Half an hour later, at 11.26, as the leading ship, *Culloden*, neared the Spanish main body containing two bunches of great three-deckers towering in the haze he made Howe's signal that he intended to pass through

the enemy's line to engage from leeward; at the same time he ordered an alteration of course a point to windward, reinforcing it a few minutes later with a signal to haul the wind (point even closer). Cordova, confronted with the British line now set on a collision course with his main body, was forced to give up any idea he may have had about joining his separated group; he also hauled up closer to the wind. His inexperienced captains, apparently unable to form line, bunched together, their ships three or four deep in places, rolling to a heavy swell as they awaited the onslaught.

The *Culloden* and the leading Spanish ships opened fire at 11.30. Troubridge, in compliance with Jervis' last signals, was steering up so close to their confused throng, three of whom had now left Cordova and were bearing down to join the group to leeward, that his first lieutenant thought they must go aboard one of the group if they held their course. 'Can't help it,' Troubridge replied. 'Let the weakest fend off!' As his guns' crews ran their pieces out for a second double-shotted broadside, they saw their enemy opposite numbers throw themselves prostrate on deck – a long-established custom in the Spanish service. An observer in one of the British frigates to leeward noted with admiration how rapidly the *Culloden*'s guns crashed out 'as if by second's watch in the silence of a port Admiral's inspection'. The three-decker *Blenheim*, following in her wake, soon added her fire and she was shortly followed by the *Prince George* and *Orion*, then two more 74's, and the seventh in line, the *Victory*. As the fleets sailed past each other on opposite tacks the ships came into action soon after one another and within a quarter of an hour the smoke and thunder of repeated broadsides had spread from the van to the centre of the British fleet, obscuring Jervis' view; before noon the last ship in the British line was warmly engaged.

By this time the *Culloden*'s guns were silent as she had run down past the last of the Spaniards to windward. Troubridge was peering back through the smoke for a glimpse of the *Victory*'s halyards, anxious for a signal which would allow him to go about and get into the battle again on the other tack. Every second that passed was taking him further from the Spanish as they sailed northwards. His men were standing by the braces and bowlines, sheets and tacks; his own acknowledgement and repeating flags were already hoisted but rolled up with a stop to prevent them breaking out. Soon after twelve o'clock he saw a hoist rising through the *Victory*'s rigging; before the flags had broken he had confirmed by the colours showing around the rolls that they were '80' – 'Tack in succession'. As they reached the top and fluttered out, he called to his own signal lieutenant, 'Break the stop!' and in the same

breath, 'Down with the helm!' The wheel was eased over – gradually so as not to take way off the ship. 'Helm's a-lee!'

'Fore sheet, fore-top-bowline, jib and staysail sheets – *Let go*!'

The headsails shivered; the bows swung to starboard. 'Off tacks and sheets!'

Aboard the flagship Jervis was ecstatic. 'Look – look at Troubridge there! He tacks his ship to battle as if the eyes of all England were upon him. And would to God they were,' he added, 'for they

Jervis' flagship, *Victory*, backs yards to rake the Spanish *Salvador del Mundo*. The main body of the Spanish fleet can be seen making off to the north, and Collingwood's *Excellent* is engaging the *San Ysidro* (with topmasts shot away).

would see him to be what I know him – and by Heavens, sir, as the Dons will soon feel him!'

The *Culloden* came round to bring the wind fine on the starboard bow; 'Mainsail haul!' Teams of waisters on the quarterdeck ran away with the braces for the main and mizen yards which – helped by the wind on the forward sides of their sails – swung round smartly. The wheel was eased amidships as she pointed dead into the wind, then swung over to the other direction as she lost way. 63

The pressure of the wind on the foresails, still braced for the previous, starboard tack and flat aback against the mast, pushed the heavy bows further off to starboard, helped by the reversed rudder as she fell very slowly astern. Gradually she brought the wind broader on the larboard bow. 'Let go and haul!' The forward tacks were let fly and the fore yards braced round like the after yards for the new tack; the wheel was eased as the sails filled, and within five minutes she was gathering way again after the Spanish whose rear ships were now nearly three quarters of a mile away to the north. Astern of him the *Blenheim* and *Prince George* were heading into the wind at different stages of their tacks.

Meanwhile six of the Spanish group to leeward led by their Vice-Admiral in the huge three-decker, *Principe d'Asturias*, had also come about and were making a bold attempt to take the British line between two fires or pass through or astern of it to join their main body. They had the misfortune to fetch the *Victory* just as she was about to tack in succession to the ships ahead of her; Jervis had his main topsail backed so that he lay right across the line of advance of the Spanish admiral who held on a collision course until, inside fifty yards, his nerve cracked. He ordered the helm down so suddenly that his raw crew, confused and panic-stricken, failed to put a hand to the braces or bowlines as the ship rounded into the wind. The slapping of the loose canvas was soon drowned in the thunder of the *Victory*'s broadside, double-shotted from three decks, shivering and breaking through the *Principe*'s bows. The Spaniards answered bravely as the turn brought their own broadside to bear, but the guns were angled so high that even at that close range most of the shot went through the rigging. As she fell off in complete confusion with the yards still angled for the larboard tack the *Victory*'s gunners had time to send two more raking broadsides into her quarter and stern which left her decks a shambles. At last she squared her yards and bore off, many of the other Spanish ships following in some disorder. Jervis had been on the poop during this time to get a clearer view of the rest of his fleet. While he was there a ball had carried off the head of a Marine and Jervis, standing near by, had been covered from hat to breeches by blood and brains. The ship's captain, seeing him in this condition, rushed up in alarm; Jervis, wiping blood from his mouth, said quietly, 'I am not at all hurt. But do, George, try if you can get me an orange.'

The British fleet was now in two distinct divisions: five of the six ships which had been ahead of the *Victory* – one, the *Colossus*, had lost her fore yards and had been forced to wear instead of tack – were on the port tack with all sail set in chase of the Spanish main body, and the *Culloden* had already caught up with the stragglers and was in action again. The British centre, led by the *Victory*, was now tacking to follow the van, while the rear ships were still coming southwards on the starboard tack, exchanging fire with the last of the Spanish to windward. It was at this point that Nelson in the *Captain*, third ship from the rear, saw that Cordova, most of whose ships had stretched well past the British rear, was leading off downwind across the tail of the British line to rejoin his separated ships to leeward. With a characteristic appreciation of the best thing to do Nelson ordered the helm up and wore the *Captain* out of the line so as to place her across the Spanish admiral's course, accomplishing the manoeuvre with such precision that Cordova in the gigantic four-decker, *Santissima Trinidad* – the largest ship in the world – together with two supporting three-deckers of 112 guns each, and one 80, all hauled up to the wind and resumed their former heading to the north. The little *Captain* was almost immediately supported by the *Culloden* as she fought her way up the Spanish body, and after some little time the *Blenheim* came up between them and the towering Spanish castles – 'which gave us a respite and sickened the Dons'.

Jervis, far from being annoyed that his desperate commodore should act on his own initiative, had seen the merit of the action immediately, and made a general signal for all ships to come to the wind on the larboard tack – instead of waiting to tack in succession. So the last remnants of order broke up as each captain went about and chose an opponent to steer for or a consort to support. By this time, about 1.30, the action was reaching a climax around the *Santissima Trinidad* and the *Captain*. To observers in one of the British frigates to leeward of this fierce mêlée as more of the British van ships came up and the cannonade reached a crescendo of fury, 'the superiority of the British fire over that of the enemy, and its effects on the enemy's hulls and sails were so evident that we in the frigate no longer hesitated to pronounce a glorious termination to the contest'.

It was at this point that the last British ship, the *Excellent*, commanded by one of Nelson's closest friends, Cuthbert Collingwood, made a devastating close-range assault on several of the Spaniards which had already been damaged in the mêlée. Collingwood was a stern and silent disciplinarian in Jervis' mould, but without such a harsh edge to his character, who had worked his guns' crews up to a rapidity of fire probably unequalled at that date. 'No sportsman ever hits a partidge without aiming at it; and skill is acquired by repeated attempts. It is the same thing in every art; unless you aim

The 74-gun *Captain* (Commodore Nelson), her foremast shot away and her rigging so cut up as to render her unmanageable, engages the 80-gun *San Nicolas* (with the three-decker *San Josef* close on the other side).

at perfection you will never attain it, but frequent attempts will make it easy.' As he tacked in response to Jervis' order to come to the wind on the larboard tack he fetched up not far astern of the van mêlée, some way ahead of the *Victory* and the rest of the centre and rear which had followed her. Consequently he soon came up with the ships which had been supporting Cordova, and had dropped astern out of the mêlée; the first was a three-decker, *Salvador del Mundo*.

'We were not farther from her when we began than the length of our garden. Her colours soon came down, and her fire ceased. I hailed and asked if she had surrendered; and when by signs I understood that they had, I left her.'

He sailed on, leaving her to be taken in possession by one of the ships astern, but looking back a few minutes later he was annoyed to see that she had re-hoisted her colours and was in action again. By this time he had come up with a Spanish 74, also damaged; he

66

ranged up 'so close alongside that a man might jump from one ship to the other. Our fire carried all before it; and in ten minutes she hauled down her colours.' Having been deceived once, he insisted that this one hoist British colours before he passed on up the line to where the *Captain*, her fore mast shot away, her rigging so cut up as to render her unmanageable, was still engaged with the 80-gun *San Nicolas*, which had the three-decker *San Josef* close by on the other (windward) side.

'My good friend (Nelson) had been long engaged with those ships and I came happily to his relief, for he was dreadfully mauled.'

He ranged up between the *Captain* and the *San Nicolas*, so close to the latter 'you could not put a bodkin between us', and much of the shot from his overheated guns went straight through the *Nicolas* into the *San Josef* beyond; in their efforts to get clear the two Spaniards fell aboard each other. As their fire ceased Colling- wood passed on to the *Santissima Trinidad* – 'such a ship as I never saw before'. Although his rigging was so damaged by this time that he could not get as close as he wished, he poured in fire, soon supported by Saumarez in the *Orion*. The *Santissima* had been closely engaged with various ships, notably the three-decker *Blen- heim*, for an hour and a half already, and it was not long before she lost her fore and mizen masts and wallowed, a virtual wreck, in the swell.

Meanwhile Nelson, his ship so crippled as to be useless for moving upwind, decided to take possession of the *San Nicolas* by boarding. His wheel had been shot away, but he ordered the helm to be hauled to starboard with tackles, luffing the *Captain* up until her spritsail yard caught in the mizen rigging of the Spaniard as she and the *San Josef* drifted leeward together. Nelson's former first lieutenant, Berry, now promoted and awaiting a ship to command, led the boarders over the beak into the Spaniard's mizen chains, while one of a company of soldiers doing duty for Marines leapt into the *Captain*'s fore chains, smashed the enemy's quarter gallery window and jumped in. Nelson restrained the ship's captain from following but was unable to stop himself; he clambered in with a sailor and a number of other soldiers and they swarmed through the great cabin firing at a few Spaniards who resisted, thence up to the quarterdeck where they met Berry and his men hauling down the colours. The Spanish captain, dying of wounds, handed Nelson his sword; a score more Spaniards had been killed in the assault and seven of the boarding party, with another ten wounded. Nelson led the rest along the larboard gangway to the forecastle, then as musket fire started from the stern of the great *San Josef*, still locked alongside,

he called for more men from the *Captain* and ordered them into the
three-decker. As he was being helped across the main chains by
Berry a Spanish officer looked over the quarterdeck rail above, and
called out that they surrendered.

> And on the quarterdeck of a Spanish 1st rate, extravagant as the story
> may seem, did I receive the swords of the vanquished Spaniards; which
> as I received I gave to Wm Fearney, one of my bargemen, who put them
> with the greatest *sang froid* under his arm. I was surrounded by Captain
> Berry, Lt. Pearson of the 69th, John Sykes, John Thomson, Francis Cook,
> all old Agamemnons, and several other brave seamen and soldiers; thus
> fell these ships.

By this time, about 3.30, the three-decker which had struck
originally to Collingwood had received further punishment and
struck to the *Victory*, which then sailed on, in a little while passing
the *Captain* locked with her two huge prizes; the flagship's company
lined the side roaring huzzas. As British frigates took all four prizes
in tow and one of their boats carried Nelson, smoke-blackened, with
tattered uniform and half his cocked hat shot away, across to the
Victory, the *Santissima Trinidad* at last submitted, first showing a
white flag to Saumarez in the *Orion*, then hoisting British colours
over her own. She had resisted against successive British ships,
usually more than one at a time, for over three hours, had crippled
one of her earlier opponents, the *Blenheim*, and killed or wounded
sixty of her company; now with over two hundred killed or

68

wounded amidst the wreck of her gun decks and with only the stump of her mainmast left above the bulwarks, Cordova recognised defeat. But Saumarez was unable to take advantage of his spectacular prize. A group of Spanish ships, including two three-deckers which had taken little part in the action so far, had worn around in support of their chief; two others bore down on the crippled *Captain*, now parted from her prizes, and a group from the separated Spanish lee division was sailing up to attack the *Colossus* which had lost her fore yards and become separated from the rest of the fleet earlier. Jervis recalled his scattered fleet with a signal to form line ahead in close order, then wore to support his two crippled ships and cover the prizes. This released the *Santissima*; she lowered her British colours and was taken in tow northwards into the main body of the Spanish fleet.

As dusk fell most of the Spaniards were standing away to the north on the larboard tack, the British line lying to on the starboard tack, shielding their four prizes; the ships' companies, despite exhaustion, were working on the torn gear aloft, splicing or reeving new ropes, fishing spars or sending up new ones from the spares kept between the gangways. Jervis kept the fleet compact all that night, and the following morning, when a large ship under tow, thought to be the *Santissima*, was made out on the horizon, refused to allow any ships to chase; the Spanish held the position of initiative to windward and could renew the contest with their still greatly superior force at any time. In fact this was their last concern; they ran for Cadiz, which had been their destination all along.

The victory off Cape St Vincent was held in the triumphant fleet, and when the news reached England, to be 'in all its circumstances, first and unparalleled in naval history'. For such a numerically inferior force to drive its opponents off in disarray and capture four prizes including two first-rates was something new in naval warfare. Jervis had predicted victory; prior to the action he had taken one of his captains into his stern gallery and pointing to his ships had said, 'Notwithstanding the disparity of force, my dear Lord Mark, with such stuff as I have about me, I shall attack them – and England shall hear of them.' But he had not expected such a victory. On the following day he wrote a memorandum to all his captains: 'No language I am possessed of can convey the high sense I entertain of the exemplary conduct of the flag officers, captains, officers, seamen, marines and soldiers embarked on board every ship of the squadron I have the honour to command.'

The ships which, by their position in the van or extreme rear of the line or by the initiative of their commanders, had borne the brunt of the close and decisive part of the action, were the *Culloden* (which had fifty-seven casualties), the *Blenheim* (sixty-one), *Prince George* (fifteen) and *Captain* (eighty casualties). But it is significant that all four Spanish ships which were captured had suffered a devastatingly close-range assault from the *Excellent* (twenty-three casualties), and in every case this had been the immediate cause of their submission – although all had previously suffered from the *Captain* and the van ships. The others of the van division, the *Orion* (none killed, nine wounded) and the *Irresistible* (nineteen casualties), played their part after the Spanish fire had been beaten down during the first close mêlée. Neither the *Victory* herself (one killed, five wounded) nor any other ships reached double figures in casualties. By contrast the *San Nicolas* lost 144 killed and fifty-nine wounded, and the casualties in the Spanish fleet as a whole have been variously estimated between one thousand and two thousand – probably nearer the lower figure; the four prizes together suffered nearly seven hundred, Cordova's flagship over two hundred.

The most spectacular incident, and the one on which most interest fastened, was Nelson's extraordinary daring, moral and physical, in placing his 74 across the Spanish admiral's line of advance. An army officer on one of the frigates to leeward declared, 'The contest in which the Commodore was thus engaged appeared to be so unequal, and the contrast between the *Captain*, a small 74-gun ship, and the gigantic ships of the enemy, was so preposterous that we could, at the moment, only view the proceeding of Nelson as rash and perilous in the extreme.' Although this view of his initiative was suggested by a few other captains even after its success in the battle, Jervis himself would not hear criticism. Nelson described his reception by the admiral on the quarterdeck of the *Victory* at the close of the action: 'having embraced me, he said he could not sufficiently thank me, and used every kind expression which could not fail to make me happy. N.B. There is a saying in the fleet too flattering for me to omit telling – viz. "Nelson's patent bridge for boarding Ist rates."'

The little Commodore, whose step to Rear-Admiral had actually been gazetted before the action, had achieved the 'name' he had craved so long. As one officer who talked to him immediately after the battle noted:

> The attainment of public honours, and an ambition to be distinguished above his fellows, were his master passions. His conduct was constantly actuated by these predominant feelings ... If such pre-eminent talents as those of this extraordinary man could be purchased so cheaply, the English nation, and indeed Europe, situated as she then was, had only to approve and applaud his moderation.

Nelson's vanity, unaffected and ingenuously dependent on good opinions, was soon to be humbled. For the moment he tasted fulfilment, writing to his wife:

> Commodore Nelson's receipt for making an Olla Podrida: Take a Spanish 1st rate and an 80 gunship and after well *battering* and *basting* them for an hour keep throwing in your *force balls*, and be sure to let these be well *seasoned*. Your *fire* must never slacken for a moment, but must be kept up as brisk as possible during the whole time so soon as you perceive your Spaniards to be well stewed and blended together you must then throw your own ship on board the two decker back your spritsail yard to her mizen mast then skip in to her quarter gallery window sword in hand …

And a fortnight after the action, as the fleet arrived back in Lisbon, he wrote to his wife: 'The more I think of our late action, the more I am astonished; it absolutely appears a dream.'

The mighty *Santissima Trinidad* of 132 guns, the largest ship in the world, across whose course Nelson placed the 74-gun *Captain*.

71

Chapter 3

Mutiny!
and Camperdown

The news of St Vincent was received ecstatically in Britain. With her bullion drained in the vain attempt to keep European armies in the field against France, her national debt higher than it had ever been and her credit lower, with her last major ally, Austria, crumbling away under Bonaparte's attack across northern Italy and about to sue for peace, with Ireland ready to rise against British rule and armies for the invasion of Ireland waiting at Brest and in the Texel, with Spanish squadrons to reinforce the covering French and Dutch fleets expected at any moment – in such dark times such a victory against apparently insuperable odds glowed with extraordinary brilliance. Whatever else failed, the Navy was invincible.

The surge of pride had scarcely time to calm when news came from Portsmouth so shocking as wholly to eclipse the triumph and all the disasters on land that had preceded it: the Channel Fleet refused to weigh anchor. The fleet on which the safety and independence of the country depended, more at this hour than at any time in her history, was in open mutiny. The danger was so extravagant it was difficult to comprehend.

It had been brewing for several months – perhaps years. Looking back the Lords of Admiralty recognised there had been indications; clear as they were in hindsight, at the time they had not seemed anything out of the ordinary run of complaints and petitions with which sailors, aggrieved by unjust or brutal punishments, rotten food, lapsed wages, relieved their feelings to a higher authority. The latest petitions had been addressed to Lord Howe – 'The Sailors' Friend'. Howe had given up active command of the Channel Fleet long since, and had been taking the waters in Bath in early March 1797 when he had received four petitions from four different Channel Fleet ships, including his old flagship, *Queen Charlotte*; later that month several more had arrived from other ships evidently posted between 7 and 11 March while the fleet was cruising. All begged him to lay before the Lords of Admiralty a particular grievance that sailors' pay had not risen when soldiers' pay had been increased two years back, nor had it kept pace with increased prices since the start of the war. They pointed out that their rate of nineteen shillings a month, twenty-two shillings and sixpence for able seamen, had been established during the reign of King Charles II – in fact it was earlier, during the Commonwealth – 'since when the cost of living has almost doubled and the cost of slops raised by 30 per cent'. The difficulties this imposed, especially on those with families, were aggravated by the feeling of

Unlike the mutiny at Spithead which was remarkable for the discipline imposed by the sailors' leaders, the Nore Mutiny soon degenerated into violence and lynch law; here a sailor is being 'ducked' – hoisted to the yardarm and dropped into the sea repeatedly, 'til scarce any signs of life remain'.

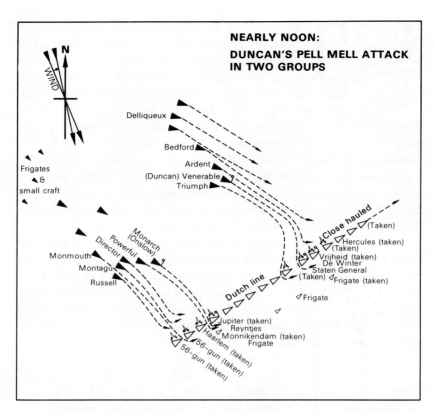

NEARLY NOON:

DUCAN'S PELL MELL ATTACK
IN TWO GROUPS

N

WIND

Delliqueux

Bedford

Ardent
(Duncan) Venerable
Triumph

Frigates
&
small craft

Monarch
(Onslow)

Powerful

Director

Monmouth

Montagu

Russell

Dutch line

Close hauled

(Taken)

Hercules (taken)
(Taken)
Vrijheid (taken)
De Winter
Staten General
(Taken)
Frigate (taken)

Frigate

Jupiter (taken)
Reyntjes
Monnikendam (taken)
Frigate

Haarlem (taken)
56-gun (taken)
56-gun (taken)

Map 4
Opening of the Battle off
Camperdown, 11
October 1797.

injustice that soldiers should now be paid one shilling a day.
Soldiers! Yet for centuries *sailors* had been recognised as England's
bulwark and pride! As the petitions claimed, 'They being fully as
loyal to their Sovereign and as courageous as any in His Majesty's
Service, as your Lordship can witness who so often led them to
victory and glory, and by whose manly exertions the British flag
rides triumphant in every quarter of the globe.'

There was another rankling irritation too, although not expressed
in the petitions; this was about the 'Bounty' paid to those who enlisted voluntarily in the Service. The traditional method of meeting
the manpower shortage resulting from the enormous increase of
ships in commission during a war was to send parties aboard in-
coming merchantmen and into seaport towns to capture and 'press'
into service any able-bodied men unfortunate enough to fall into
their clutches. This had not met the enormous naval expansion of
the present war, and in 1795 Pitt had introduced the Quota Acts:
each county and large town in the kingdom was required to provide a number of men for the Navy, its 'quota' being fixed according

to population. Still wastage by disease, desertion and battle, together with the increased responsibilities of the Navy as its enemies multiplied, made it necessary to entice volunteers with ever-increasing 'Bounties' – up to £60 in some cases. A naval surgeon wrote:

> These extraordinary occurrences did not pass unnoticed by the seamen. The sensations of disgust which they excited were pointed and strong. 'What,' they said, 'shall these tailors and cobblers be receiving their £50 while we are doomed to take £5?' This business was never forgotten, the wound festered and had its share in producing the discontents of 1797.

There were other grievances too – but undoubtedly low pay was the trigger. The same naval surgeon wrote:

> The founders of the mutiny were men about the middle age, married and had children. Their families were daily claiming relief from them; provisions for the two preceding years 1795 and 1796 had been enormously high, and they found themselves starving. These families contrasted their situation with that of other more fortunate seamen who escaped impressment, and were receiving from the merchants £4 and £5 a month, while seamen in the King's ships got 22/6. How was it possible for men placed in such circumstances to be insensible of their wives and families?

Howe, far away in Bath, suffering severely from gout, failed to recognise the danger signs in the petitions. The early ones, he thought, had all been written by one person, disguising his hand; he suspected that all the rest had been inspired by this same trouble-maker. Nevertheless he did write to the Admiralty suggesting that enquiries be made about any signs of discontent in the fleet, and when he went to London at the end of March, he gave the petitions to their Lordships. Later the Channel Fleet returned from cruising and anchored in Spithead. The sailors were expecting replies to their several petitions but Howe, having handed over responsibility, did not write, nor did the Admiralty give any indication that they were giving the matter thought; they were not. As the days passed and the feeling grew in the fleet that the real and deeply-felt injustice had been dismissed with scorn, preparations were made in secret for concerted action to force their case to the attention of the Admiralty – and the country at large. In each ship petty officers and experienced able seamen elected two delegates to represent them, and concerted preparations with other ships during the Sunday afternoon ship-visiting that was allowed in harbour. New petitions were prepared, this time addressed to the Secretary of the Admiralty and to the leader of the Opposition

The Channel Fleet lying
at Spithead; in the
foreground the flagship
Queen Charlotte.

in Parliament; directly these had been sent they meant to take charge of the fleet and keep control until they received satisfaction.

> The signal will be first made by the *Queen Charlotte*. The first signal is the Union Jack at the main with two guns fired: this is for taking charge and sending the officers and women out of every ship. The second signal is a red flag at the mizen topmasthead, and two guns; this is to send a speaker from every ship …

76 Before long several officers learnt of the preparations from in-

formers and others who did not trouble to hide their discontent, and by 14 April the Commander-in-Chief, Lord Bridport, and the Admiral in charge at Portsmouth had both warned the Admiralty that the sailors were preparing to refuse duty until their wages were increased; the mutiny was to begin on Tuesday next at a signal from the *Queen Charlotte*. The Admiralty response was to attempt to split the ships by ordering one division under Admiral Gardner to drop down to St Helens, and the whole fleet to prepare for sea.   77

Bridport knew the orders would not be obeyed, but he had to give them, and did so on Easter Sunday, 16 April. This was two days before the outbreak was due to start, but the men were in no mood to be diverted, and Gardner had scarcely given the order for his division to weigh when the fore rigging of his ships swarmed with men roaring cheers. Soon the cheering had spread throughout the fleet. The mutiny had begun. Boats put out and two delegates from every ship were rowed to the *Queen Charlotte*, where they met in the great cabin formerly occupied by Lord Howe, and drew up a list of regulations for the good order of the fleet while they remained in charge.

An account of these incidents reached the Admiralty at midnight. After an initial refusal to understand the solidarity of the men, hence the unique situation with which he was faced, the young First Lord, Spencer, made hurried preparations for members of the Board to accompany him to Portsmouth; they left London by coach in the early evening of the 17th, and rattling through the night reached the dockyard town by noon the following day; immediately Lord Bridport, Gardner and the other Admirals were summoned to a meeting at the Fountain Inn. The result of the impromptu Board was a 'project', or compromise by which ordinary seamen would get three shillings, able seamen four shillings more a month. This was to be put to the committee of delegates.

At this time the delegates were drawing up a petition asking – in addition to a pay rise equal to the soldiers' – for fresh meat and vegetables to be supplied in port, shore leave allowed in port, an end to the system whereby ships' pursers kept for their own profit two ounces in every pound of the sailors' nominal rations, an end to the iniquitous system of stopping a man's pay directly he became sick or wounded, an end to embezzlement of the supplies provided for sick and wounded, and 'if any ship has real grievances to complain of, we hope your Lordships will readily redress them, as far as is in your power ...' These were all reasonable requests even by the harsh standards of the day. They made no mention of the various brutal punishments seamen were subject to – except in the final plea for Admiralty redress for 'real grievances' which probably referred to the minority of sadistic or totally insensitive officers who punished for their own satisfaction or in their cups. Nor was any mention made of the notoriously unfair distribution of prize money, by which sailors received a few pounds while commanders-in-chief made small fortunes. Both abuses had already been brought to the Admiralty's attention by *officers*. The delegates were also showing moderation and political judgement in other ways. Determined to present their case in the best light and if possible to carry the public with them, they had made it clear that at the first appearance of an enemy fleet they would call off the mutiny and sail in defence of the country – which immediately won them sympathy – and they had persuaded the crews of two ships required for convoy duty to sail, despite their desire to stay with the mutiny. They had forbidden liquor to be taken aboard lest the men become riotous and had hung nooses from the yardarms to make it clear that there would be no relaxation of discipline while they were in charge. The officers, meanwhile, were treated with courtesy, the usual formalities were observed for piping captains and admirals aboard, and all duties were carried on as normal for ships in harbour. Red flags in place of the admirals' or the captains' pennants at the ships' mastheads were almost the only outward signs of the changed authority.

Their reception of Lord Spencer's 'project', which neither answered their plea for equal pay nor mentioned other grievances, was equally moderate and firm; they simply sent the 'humble petition' they had been preparing, which listed all the points they had agreed.

When this was brought to the Fountain Inn, the members of the Board at dinner were still under the impression that the mutiny was the desperate act of a few troublemakers, and deciding that they could not admit any of the points without opening the floodgates to even greater demands, concocted more schemes to separate the ships and isolate those containing the ringleaders. The following morning they met the admirals again, and sixteen captains of the fleet; these at last brought them to some realisation of the feeling that ran through *all* the men, and reluctantly Spencer abandoned the various plans for slipping cables by stealth; very reluctantly he took the officers' advice to meet the pay demands in full. The new 'project' which he drew up also conceded the sixteen-ounce pound for provisions and continuous pay for the wounded and sick. When this was read out to the ships' companies many seemed prepared to return to duty, but all insisted that the delegates should make the decision. These sober men, assembled as usual in the Great Cabin of the *Queen Charlotte*, were almost satisfied.

But we beg leave to remind your Lordships, that it is a firm resolution that, until the flour (instead of fresh provisions) in port be removed, the vegetables and pensions augmented, the grievances of private ships redressed, an Act passed, and His Majesty's gracious pardon for the Fleet now lying at Spithead be granted, that the Fleet will not lift an anchor: and this is the total and final answer.

Directly he heard of their determination Spencer boarded his coach, again travelling through the night to London, where he met the Prime Minister and the Chancellor, and after a Cabinet meeting all three set out for Windsor for an audience with the King; at the Castle a royal pardon was written out, signed and rushed to the printers, from whence a hundred copies were despatched by express to Portsmouth, arriving early in the morning of the following day. They were read out and displayed on board the ships of the fleet and the delegates, some reluctantly for there were still no formal concessions on fresh meat and vegetables, agreed to return to duty. The nooses and the red flags were hauled down, admirals' flags run up and ships' companies manned the yards, announcing the end of the mutiny as they had begun it with three hearty cheers.

It was a triumphant conclusion for the delegates whose moderate demands, firm control and outstanding judgement had kept the potentially savage passions of the more brutalised and rebellious from turning what had been in effect a strike into red mutiny. They had won all their major points and even in those matters which had not been conceded had drawn the Admiralty's attention to the urgent need for reform.

Immensely able and wise as they were, the delegates could not command events outside their own fleet. In the country at large, where there were numberless secret cells of Republican sympathisers with the French Revolution, with the Irish cause, with Catholic emancipation, Parliamentary reform and all the democratic theories that had spread throughout Europe and America, the mutiny had been seized upon as a gift to bring down the government. Underground presses were running off handbills and broadsheets by the hundred, and these were being clandestinely distributed to units of the fleet around the coasts in Plymouth, Portsmouth, the Nore and Yarmouth, as incitements to the sailors to stand up for their 'natural rights'. Irish secret societies were among the most active. Already the previous year a proclamation had been addressed to all Irishmen serving in the British Navy – who formed more than ten per cent of the total – stating that Ireland was now at war with England in defence of her rights; they were, therefore, no longer subjects of the King of England. Together with general provocation to treason by the secret societies there was a particular campaign to convince the sailors that the government had hoodwinked the Spithead mutineers and intended, now that the fleet had returned to duty, to go back on its promises; they were helped in this aim by Opposition speeches in the Lords. With such goads, with their own real grievances, with large numbers of pressed men naturally disgruntled by their confinement, with only slightly smaller numbers of 'Quota men', some of whom had been sent into the Service straight from jail, others from magistrates' courts or debtors' prisons, some with education, most with far more worldly knowledge than the sailors, closed up as they were in their own tight community, the majority *despised* by the real sailors – with such an explosive mixture and the successful example of Spithead it was not surprising that by the end of April there was an outbreak of mutiny at Plymouth, rumblings at St Helens where the greater part of the Channel Fleet awaited a fair wind to sail for Brest, preparations for mutiny at the Nore and an apparently spontaneous outbreak

Admiral Duncan, who blockaded the Dutch fleet in the Texel with just two ships of the line during the mutinies.

aboard the *Venerable*, flagship of Admiral Adam Duncan, Commander-in-Chief of the North Sea Fleet at Yarmouth. The crew surged up the fore rigging and roared out three cheers, which had been the signal for the Spithead affair to begin. The cheers were taken up by one other ship near by, the *Nassau*.

Duncan was not a man to be daunted. He had braved a rioting mob in Edinburgh singlehanded five years back; in ability, resolution, contempt for danger and benevolent firmness with his men, whose interest he always had at heart, he was the equal of Lord Howe; in appearance he was the most impressive flag officer in the Service. A Scot from Dundee, his size and strength were 'almost gigantic ... six foot four inches in height and of a corresponding breadth. When a young lieutenant walking through the streets of Chatham, his grand figure and handsome face attracted crowds of admirers.' At sixty-six, his strength, 'manly and athletic form' and the 'singularly handsome', benevolent features with high forehead now crowned with snow-white hair were all remarkably preserved. So far fortune had denied him the chance of great distinction; although he had served with most of the glittering names of the century, Hawke and Boscawen in his early years, as a protégé of Keppel, when he had led a storming party at the siege of Moro Castle armed only with a heavy stick, with Rodney's fleet in the War of American Independence, leading the larboard division during Howe's relief of Gibraltar, by quirks of fate he had been absent from the great fleet actions. In 1795, after some years on half pay, he had been appointed to command the new North Sea Fleet raised to mark the Dutch fleet as Holland (the new Batavian Republic) re-entered the war on the French side. Again the chances of battle passed him by; despite the most diligent blockading he had failed to bring the Dutch fleet to action. He had been offered the Mediterranean command, but had turned it down, preferring to keep watch over the Dutch as the invasion forces assembled.

When the men crowded the fore rigging of his flagship in Yarmouth Roads on Sunday, 30 April 1797, he assembled his officers immediately and had the Marines paraded, armed, on the quarterdeck and poop – 'Major Trollope, the subalterns and privates of Marines were under arms as quick as thought' – then strode along the gangway to the forecastle with a thunderous expression and demanded to know the meaning of the demonstration. He was greeted with awed silence. A few of the men 'appearing more forward than the rest', he resisted a temptation to unsheath his sword and run the nearest through, instead ordering them aft to the poop. Afterwards he had all hands assembled on the quarterdeck and interrogated the five leaders before them; they had little to say for themselves – 'as their friends at Spithead had done so, they thought no harm, and they wished to know when their increased pay and provisions was to commence'. Duncan told them that the Act to increase their pay was going through Parliament, and warned them of the consequences and the enormity of their crime. Finally he pardoned them all and sent them about their duties.

The following Sunday he assembled them all again. 'My lads – you have had a week to reflect on what happened on Sunday last, and I doubt not will agree with me in thinking your conduct highly improper. I know many of you think so.' He went on to warn them against the 'few designing men, and those not the best characters', who had led them to it; he would keep an eye on those men himself. But he had heard it rumoured that the ship's company would refuse to put to sea. 'As a matter of that kind should not be doubtful, I ask you, and I shall ask every ship in the fleet, is that your determination?'

For reply the spokesman for the ship's company said they were sincerely ashamed of their rash step; 'and we humbly implore your honour's pardon with hearts full of gratitude and tears in our eyes for the offence we have given to the worthiest of commanders who has proved a father to us'.

Duncan reinforced the moment with an appeal to their patriotism: the country, he said, was surrounded by enemies, but they had nothing to fear if the fleet maintained the 'shining character it had won for itself', and he urged them to think of the regard they owed their country and their families.

You see me now grown grey with fifty-one years' service. In every ship I had the honour to command I have endeavoured to do justice both to the public and to the men I commanded and have often been flattered with particular marks of their regard; and I still hope, in spite of all that has happened, this ship's company will not have lost their confidence in me. Both my officers and me are always ready to redress any supposed grievances when asked in a proper manner.

He ended, 'God bless you all, and may He always have us under His gracious protection and make us better men. Go to your worthy pastor and hear what he has to say.'

Duncan exercised his personal authority in similar manner on each of his ships during the next few days as the situation became ugly with news that mutiny had broken out again in the Channel Fleet and at the Nore, and at first he succeeded in holding back the contagion. When one ship, the *Adamant*, did break out a week later he went aboard her immediately and after saying to the assembled   83 hands that he would much rather acquire their love than incur their fear, threatened to put to death with his own hand 'the first man who shall display the slightest sign of rebellious conduct'. In the ensuing silence he asked if there was anyone who presumed to dispute his authority or that of his officers. When one man stepped forward he seized him by the collar and swung him over the side of the ship, dangling him there with one arm.

'My lads – look at this fellow – he who dares to deprive me of command of the fleet!'

The Adamants remained loyal thereafter.

The first blood in the new outbreaks occurred aboard the *London*, flagship of Admiral Colpoys in the Channel Fleet. On Sunday, 7 May, she was lying at Spithead, separated from most of the rest of the ships, when her captain reported to the admiral, 'Everything appears as wrong as ever with the fleet lying at St Helens. The boats are assembling and the yard ropes reeved as formerly.' The immediate cause of this repetition of 16 April was a change in the wind allowing the ships to sail; the men refused to weigh because they had become convinced that the government had no intention of honouring the agreement, but only wanted to split them up: 'If they once divide us and get us upon different stations they think they can then make their own terms.' In fact Pitt was doing his best to get the 'Seamen's Bill' through Parliament in short time. In any case, Colpoys, who had received a memorandum from the Admiralty enjoining stern measures to preserve discipline, made up his mind that the *London* would not be taken from him a second time. When it was reported that several boats were approaching from St Helens he had the lower gunports closed to prevent communication through them, sent his crews below decks, had the hatches closed and Marine sentries posted over them, and around the upper decks to prevent any mutineers coming aboard, and the officers also armed and stationed at strategic points.

However, as the boats carrying the delegates neared the ship, the men below, some full of rum, grew restive and swarmed to the ladders demanding to be allowed up; others hauled a few middle-deck guns inboard and elevated them to point up the hatchways where the Marines stood with fixed bayonets. As it became clear that they were going to rush the hatches Colpoys gave his officers and Marines permission to open fire; in the ensuing scramble and burst of musket shots the lieutenant of Marines, a midshipman, a mate and four sailors fell wounded, three severely, while one sailor lay dying from a shot from the first lieutenant, Peter Bover. Maddened, the men surged on deck past the Marines, most of whom changed sides and dropped their arms, and crying 'Blood for blood!' seized Bover, hustled him to the forecastle and prepared a yard rope for summary execution; meanwhile steadier hands among the warrant and petty officers tried to break up the mêlées and Colpoys, realising that he had lost, called to his officers to cease resistance and retired with them and two loyal Marines to the quarterdeck.

By this time the enraged group on the forecastle had a noose around Peter Bover's neck and were about to hoist him aloft, but the ship's surgeon, a trusted man, persuaded them to wait and hear what the admiral had to say. Simultaneously the delegates from St Helens climbed on board and made their way to the forecastle; one of them, named Valentine Joyce, a steady quartermaster's mate from the *Royal George*, and one of the decisive voices in the councils of the delegates, flung his arm around Bover's neck and said, 'If you hang this man you shall hang me, for I shall never quit him!' This inspired one of the Londons to call out that Bover was a brave boy. And Colpoys, who had come forward from the quarter-deck, pushed his way through the crowd to stand by Bover. He regarded Bover as one of the most promising officers he had ever met and said that his lieutenant had only obeyed orders to fire; if anyone was to blame it was himself. And as for that, he was only following recent Admiralty instructions to resist attempts at mutiny. The men were instantly alert; this seemed to confirm their worst suspicions that the Admiralty meant to go back on its word while suppressing any further attempts to gain redress. They demanded to see the instructions. Colpoys went aft again and deliberately spent a long time looking for them. When he returned passions had cooled a little; instead of hanging Bover or Colpoys, the men decided to confine them to their cabins, together with the ship's captain, until they could be tried.

At the tribunal held aboard the *Queen Charlotte* on the following day Valentine Joyce and a newly elected delegate from the *London*, an able seaman named John Fleming, defended Bover against a majority mood for vengeance. Both these men had been decisive in calming the enraged Londons the day before; now they repeated the feat with a passion and eloquence which would have been a credit to the Bar.

My brethren, your general cry is 'Blood for Blood!' Do you mean that as a compliment to us to assist us in following error after error? If so, it is a poor compliment indeed: or do you – let me ask you – think it justice? I hope not. If you do so, pray from whence do you derive the authority to sit as a court over the life of even the meanest subject?

He warned them of unquiet consciences if they presumed to take the life even of a criminal, 'much more that of a deserving and worthy gentleman who is an ornament to his profession in every respect'. Urging them to act 'in a manner worthy the character of Christians and British seamen', he ended, 'I am but a single individual among you, and before this hand of mine shall subscribe the name of Fleming to anything that may in the least tend to this gentleman's prejudice, much more to his life, I will undergo your utmost violence, and meet death with him hand in hand.'

Bover was released that evening, Colpoys and his flag captain later.

The government in London, alarmed by the fresh outbreaks and the bloodshed, and by the mutineers at St Helens sending ashore more than a hundred unpopular commissioned and warrant officers, rushed the 'Seamen's Bill' through both Houses of Parliament, speedily obtained the Royal assent, and had copies printed and sent by express to Portsmouth. The King, meanwhile, suggested that Lord Howe, long his favourite admiral, should go to the fleet as a conciliator. It was a brilliant stroke. Black Dick was still 'The Sailor's Friend'; though seventy-one years old, often crippled with gout and in excruciating pain, he set out for Portsmouth on 10 May and spent the following days with the fleet, talking with the delegates in his old cabin in the *Queen Charlotte*, being hauled up the side of every ship and speaking to the men, waving copies of a new Royal Pardon in their faces as he endeavoured to quiet their extreme suspicions of the government's good faith. Each time he seemed to be approaching a settlement there appeared to be 'some watchful agents, not yet to be traced, who neglect no opportunity to start fresh difficulties'. Perhaps the greatest difficulty was the large number of officers who had been sent ashore by the mutineers; although Howe knew it would be a most dangerous precedent to allow ships' companies to depose unpopular officers, the men would not have them back aboard, and in the end he had to agree to 107 new appointments, one admiral in place of Colpoys, four captains and twenty-nine lieutenants among them. With this obstacle out of the way, the delegates were willing to return to duty; to seal the occasion, undoubtedly the most valuable service of all that Howe had rendered his King and country, on 15 May he received the delegates on board the *Royal William* and after accepting addresses of contrition, led them in a great aquatic procession with bands and pageantry through the fleet, Valentine Joyce at Lady Howe's side. The sun brightened Royal Standards hoisted in place of the bloody red flags of mutiny. Afterwards the delegates

86

drank wine with the old admiral at the Governor's house in Portsmouth. Two days later the fleet weighed and sailed for Brest.

Commenting on his arduous negotiations, Howe described the mutineers as having 'the most suspicious, but most generous minds he thinks he ever met with in the same class of men'. Had this not been so, had there not been leaders of the exceptional quality of Joyce and Fleming and a good number of steady, moderate hands to back them up, the Admiralty's early mistakes, which had stemmed from total misunderstanding of the sailors' mood, might have proved irretrievable.

At the Nore the mutineers were led by very different men. Although they copied the system of delegates, organisation and regulations established at Spithead, they lacked restraint and, glorying in sudden power, lost sight of their objectives – if indeed they had ever been clear about them. For by the time they formulated their demands and presented them, the 'Seamen's Act' to raise their pay had been passed long since and the Channel Fleet had made its peace and sailed. Most of the points they raised were, nevertheless, very reasonable – shore leave, a fairer distribution of prize money, and shorter arrears of pay were the main ones; they added one that no government could have conceded: officers whom the crew deposed for undue severity should not be allowed to return to the ship!

However reasonable the main demands, Spencer and the Cabinet had made up their minds not to negotiate. With the Channel Fleet back to duty and Duncan preserving good order at Yarmouth, they took the line that treating with the delegates at the Nore would raise mutiny into a respectable way of airing griev-

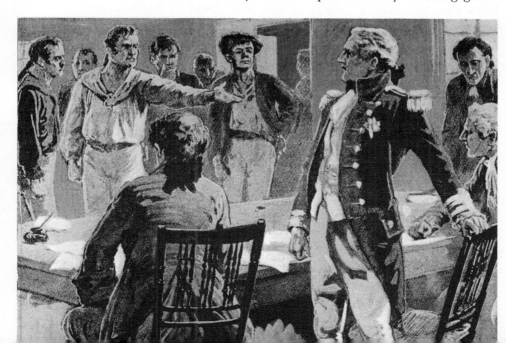

Mutiny at the Nore! The Admiralty refuse to consider the demands of the sailors' delegates.

ances. Admitting only the point about arrears of pay – the administration of which was scandalous – they refused the rest and offered free pardons to all those who returned to duty. This unceremonious rejection, far from bringing the delegates to a sense of the enormity of their crime, as the Admiralty had hoped, merely hardened them. Already drunk with their sudden authority and freedom, landing riotously each day at Sheerness and waving red flags, marching through the streets behind a band to the Chequers Inn, where they held highly charged meetings, having themselves rowed in state through the fleet, bands playing, all hands turned out to cheer – without restraints of any kind they had worked themselves and their supporters into a state of insolent euphoria. Their acknowledged leader was Richard Parker, a former warrant officer of violent and unstable temper who had been disrated for insolence during the American war, subsequently dismissed the Service, and drafted in again with the 'Quota' from a debtors' prison earlier that year. A man of good education, he had a gift for rousing oratory; styling himself 'Admiral' of 'The Floating Republic', his speeches had more in common with the demagogues of the French Revolution than with the sober leaders at Spithead.

> Shall we, who have endured the toils of a tedious, disgraceful war, be the victims of tyranny and oppression which vile, gilded, pampered knaves, wallowing in the lap of luxury, choose to load us with? Shall we, who amid the rage of tempest and the war of jarring elements, undaunted climb the unsteady cordage and totter on the topmast's dreadful height, suffer ourselves to be treated worse than the dogs of London streets? No – the age of reason has at length resolved. Long have we been endeavouring to find ourselves men. We now find ourselves so.

This picture of Nelson in 1800 by Füger gives some indication of the fascination he exerted on his contemporaries.

Overleaf View of the *Victory*'s deck from the starboard mizen rigging at the height of the Battle of Trafalgar.

With the Admiralty's refusal to talk and Parker's flamboyant oratory confirming the delegates in their defiance, the situation grew daily more dangerous. The Admiralty reinforced the garrison at Sheerness and stopped the supply of provisions to the fleet and all communication with the town in an effort to isolate and starve the mutineers out. Despite the small number of ships involved, Spencer felt that 'the welfare and almost the existence of the country may depend upon what is the event of this very important crisis', and before the end of May he was discussing the use of Duncan's fleet to suppress the mutiny. Duncan was naturally reluctant for such a distasteful duty, but was confident of his men, and told the Board, 'I do not shrink from the business if it cannot otherwise be got the better of.' The Venerables, meanwhile getting wind of the plan, wrote him a remarkable declaration of loyalty, ending, 'it would appear unnatural for us to unsheath the sword

88

against our brethren, notwithstanding we would wish to show ourselves like men in behalf of our Commander, should necessity require.'

Spencer had no sooner made up his mind to use the North Sea Fleet against the mutineers when intelligence from Holland indicated that the invasion force assembled at the Texel had embarked and was only waiting a favourable wind to put out. Duncan was directed to sail there instead. As he did so, one by one his ships were taken over by their seamen, and deserted him, some to return to Yarmouth Roads, some to the Nore, where all eventually joined the 'Floating Republic', hoisting the red flag, swelling the number of Parker's 'fleet' to twenty-four and giving unexpected new life to the mutiny. For Duncan it was the hardest moment of his life.

> To be deserted by my fleet in the face of the enemy is a disgrace which I believe never before happened to a British Admiral, nor could I have supposed it possible. Our cup is overflowing and has made us wanton. The all-wise Providence has given us this check as a warning, and I hope we shall improve by it.

Nevertheless two of the line remained loyal, his own *Venerable* and the *Adamant*, where he had extinguished a former outbreak, and with these two he proceeded to the Texel to carry out his orders to blockade the Dutch invasion force – creating thereby one of the imperishable legends of the Revolutionary War. For three days he

Opposite top Nelson on the quarterdeck of the *Victory* as she breaks the line and rakes Villeneuve's flagship at Trafalgar.

Opposite bottom Nelson's flagships.

The *Clyde* frigate, whose crew had never been wholeheartedly behind the mutiny, cuts her cables and sets sail to escape from the mutinous fleet at the Nore.

cruised off the Dutch coast, every morning looking close in to the mouth of the Texel itself, the first day wearing the flag of a Rear-Admiral of the Red at the mizen peak and hoisting a stream of signals to an imaginary main body of the fleet in the offing, the next day appearing as two private ships with captains' pennants only, making more signals, and the third day under his proper colours as an Admiral of the Blue.

On the following day he was joined by two more of the line which the Admiralty had sent, and as the wind came round to the east, fair for the Dutch to sail, he stood right in and anchored his little squadron off the outer buoy of the Texel with instructions to fight the ships till they sank; their hulls would block the exit channel. And summoning his men, he told them, 'The soundings are such that my flag will continue to fly above the water after the ship and her company have disappeared. But if we survive this duty we shall sail to the Nore and reduce those misguided men to obedience.' The men growled their approval.

The Dutch fleet of eighteen of the line with numerous frigates never put out. Not only was the army of invasion not ready, but they were convinced that Duncan's four ships were a decoy while the main body, to which he had been signalling, waited just over the horizon. On 10 June Duncan was joined by six more ships which the Admiralty had detached from the Channel Fleet, and on the 13th by a Russian squadron under orders to co-operate with him. The danger was over. Spencer wrote to congratulate him on 'making so good a countenance with your four ships as to keep the whole Dutch fleet in awe'.

Meanwhile the Admiralty policy of isolating the Nore mutineers and starving them into submission had succeeded. After a period during which the leaders had resorted to increasing violence to preserve authority over moderate elements who had come to realise they were gaining nothing, the more desperate and politically conscious threatened to take the ships to the enemy – to France or to the Texel. Already a four-day blockade of all commercial shipping on the Thames and the unruly behaviour and intemperate language of the delegates had lost them public sympathy; now they lost the support of the majority of their own people. 'We'll be damned if we leave old England whatever happens to us.' So counter-rebellions had started in individual ships. The first had been aboard the *Leopard*; after the hard core of mutineers had been overpowered with the loss of one life, she cut her cable and slipped away, unfortunately running aground and coming under fire from the rest of Parker's 'fleet' before she finally escaped. She was soon

94

Richard Parker, self-styled 'Admiral of The Floating Republic', is hanged from the yard-arm of the *Sandwich* after the collapse of the mutiny.

followed by the *Repulse*, which also came under fire for a while, although most of the guns' crews aimed wide. By 12 June, after bloody struggles on board individual ships, all but two had hauled down the red flag of mutiny, and in the evening of the 14th the last one, Parker's own *Sandwich*, submitted to the port admiral. By this time many of the ringleaders had escaped by boat, most making their way to the Continent. Parker did not; after taking a vote of his ship's company which went almost unanimously in favour of the officers, he handed over the keys of the storerooms and magazines, then led the three cheers signifying a return to duty. A week later he was tried by court martial and, inevitably, sentenced to death; on 30 June he was hoisted to the fore yardarm of the *Sandwich*. Although his conduct at the end was as admirable as most of the 95 mutineers' demands had been reasonable, he never recognised the flaws in character and practical politics which had brought him to such a different end from the Spithead leaders. 'Remember never to make yourself the busybody of the lower classes,' he said bitterly at the last. 'Whom they have exalted one moment as their demagogue, the next they will not scruple to exalt upon the gallows.'

Although more than four hundred other mutineers were court-martialled over the following months and fifty-eight were sentenced to death, the Admiralty acted wisely in pardoning the majority; eventually twenty-eight were hanged, twenty-nine imprisoned and nine flogged. The combination of severe examples and extraordinary leniency – for such dangerous times – together with the concessions made at Spithead, and a general moderation of officers' attitudes towards punishment and shore leave stemming directly from the shattering experiences at the Nore, served to bring the greater part of the fleet to order. There were isolated outbreaks on foreign stations, and some of the Channel Fleet ships harboured seditious groups who still talked of taking their vessels over to the enemy; the worst of these were sent to that formidable disciplinarian, John Jervis – now Earl of St Vincent – as he watched the Spanish fleet in Cadiz. At the first outbreaks he had the affected ships surrounded by armed launches and the ring-leaders hoisted to the yardarm by their own ship's company – a new departure in naval executions. Very soon the most disaffected were quiet and new arrivals, expecting to spread their own 'libertarian' views, even to carrying the ships to the enemy in Cadiz, were warned by their brethren in the fleet.

'Messmates take care you say nothing about all that here – for by God if old Jarvie hears ye, he'll have you dingle-dangle at the yardarm at eight o'clock tomorrow morning.'

All through that summer, while Jervis maintained a close blockade of the Spanish fleet, Duncan kept watch on the Dutch expedition in the Texel. By the middle of August the Dutch admiral, De Winter, by coincidence a man of large physique almost matching Duncan's, became convinced that the invasion project was hopeless; with the British line just outside now seventeen strong, with provisions running low from the long wait with all troops aboard, the project was abandoned. When the Admiralty learned this at the end of September Duncan was ordered back to Yarmouth to refit after his arduous sea-keeping. But anxious as ever to keep the

Dutch under observation he ordered two of the line back to the Texel on 3 October after only forty-eight hours at home; these had scarcely arrived on station when De Winter took a fleet of sixteen of the line to sea.

The Dutch cruise had no object apart from curing disaffection among the sailors, who had been idle too long, and hopefully perhaps luring isolated parts of the British fleet on to the shoal waters close off the coast. De Winter himself was against the cruise, but he had been overruled; his orders were to engage the enemy if the forces opposed were such as to give 'hope of success', to 'try and cause as much damage to the enemy as possible', to 'try and draw enemy forces as near the Harbours of the Republic as possible in conformity with rules of prudence and stategy' and to bear in mind 'how frequently Dutch Admirals have maintained the honour of the Dutch flag, even when the enemy's forces were sometimes superior to theirs'. Directly he left harbour, making south-westerly on 6 October, he was shadowed by the observation squadron, and soon receiving intelligence that Duncan had been informed of his movements and was out again in force, he made back the way he had come. Duncan reached the Texel before him; finding the anchorage empty he waited just off the coast for his return.

De Winter obliged the following morning, 11 October. The British squadron of observation, still hanging some three miles to windward of the Dutch, in this case north of them as they made north-easterly for the coast, first sighted Duncan's fleet in the north-east at daybreak, and after closing to make sure that they were British ships, fired a gun and hoisted the signal, 'Enemy in sight, bearing S × W.' Duncan, who had been tacking back and forth, put his helm up and ran down towards them. The weather was dark with squalls, the wind very fresh on the starboard quarter, the grey sea, beaten under showers of rain, lumping angrily and streaked with broken white. As they approached, the frigate *Circe*, most northerly of the observing squadron, signalled the enemy force as sixteen of the line, and before long the Dutch topsails could be made out from the flagship's fore rigging, bearing SSW; at nine o'clock Duncan signalled 'Prepare for battle.'

Twenty minutes later, as it became clear that De Winter was forming line of battle close hauled on the larboard tack, heading north-easterly, Duncan ordered his fleet to form a line of bearing NE to SW, and alter course to SSE. This brought the wind right astern and the Dutch fleet about four points ($45°$) on his starboard bow. Soon after ten o'clock, impatient to close before they reached the shoal water near the land, he altered course to south and made

97

the signal to chase, enforcing it with two guns, and following it shortly with the signal to 'engage the enemy as arriving up'. The wind, although still gusting, was easing slightly and veering to the north and within a short time the ships had shaken out the reefs in their topsails, spread t'gallants and all their courses, winged out the fore yards with studding sails, and were driving down at their best rate, the faster sailers drawing away from the rest so that the still unformed line of bearing dissolved completely into ragged groups. The sun broke fitfully on the wild scene, the heaving sea and the spray suddenly brilliant; Duncan felt he had 'never been so exalted by so exhilarating a sensation as the sight the two fleets afforded him'. He called his officers to the quarterdeck and knelt with them in prayer.

By eleven o'clock his leading ships were within two miles of the enemy, but the rest were too far extended, and with the Dutch formed in close line awaiting the attack with admirable calm, he signalled the leaders to shorten sail; shortly afterwards he made a signal for the fleet to come to the wind together on the starboard tack so that he might close up and dress the line properly. While the rear ships were still straggling towards their appointed places a brightening of the eastern horizon revealed land and the houses of the small villages of Camperdown and Egmont barely nine miles from the Dutch van – heading inshore. There was no time to be lost if he was not to be drawn into shoal water, and once again he abandoned formal tactics and ordered the fleet to put their helms up together and run down on the enemy, 'each ship to steer for and engage her opponent'. He followed this with Howe's signal to pass through the enemy line and engage from leeward.

Like Howe, he had some captains who lacked stomach for such a desperately close encounter, others who could not make out the meaning of the rash of signals they had been treated to that morning; the Scots captain of the *Belliqueux* gave up, flung his copy of the signal book on deck with an oath and cried, 'Up wi' the hel-lem and gang into the middle o't!'

So they stood downwind towards the Dutch under double-reefed topsails and foresails – although some of the smaller and slower ships spread t'gallants in an effort to keep up. Soon the rough line of bearing they had been forming while lying-to broke up into two groups; the southernmost, headed by Vice-Admiral Onslow in the 74-gun *Monarch*, closely supported by the *Powerful*, 74, just abaft his starboard beam, the *Director*, 64, and two more 74's, the *Montagu* and *Russell*, steered for the last four ships in the Dutch line, the 74-gun *Jupiter*, flagship of Rear-Admiral Reyntjes, the

68-gun *Haarlem*, and bringing up the extreme rear two small 56-gun ships; straggling in the wake of the British 74's came three 64's and a 50-gun ship – altogether nine British falling upon four Dutchmen, two of whom were no possible match for the leading 74's. To the north of this leeward division, Duncan in his 74-gun *Venerable*, closely supported by the *Triumph*, 74, on his starboard quarter and the *Ardent*, 64, on his port quarter, steered for De Winter's flagship, the 74-gun *Vrijheid*, fifth ship from the Dutch van; somewhat astern and to larboard of the *Venerable* and *Ardent* were the *Bedford*, 74, two 64's and another 50-gun ship, aiming up towards the Dutch ships ahead of the *Vrijheid*.

Thus the central six or seven ships in the Dutch line ahead of their rear flagship *Jupiter* were left unattended and a gap widened between the two groups of British ships. De Winter, seeing the peril to his rear, made the signal to shorten sail in an effort to close his centre and van to their support. He had hoped to get further inshore while Duncan formed and dressed his line, but the precipitate attack denied him the chance. He expected his ships to fight stubbornly when the British fell on them, as Dutchmen had always fought, but he could not hope for success. The numbers were equal, each with sixteen two-decked ships of the line, but against the seven 74's heading Duncan's and Onslow's onslaught he could only muster four, one in the centre away from the threatened points; he had seven 68- or 64-gun ships to match the seven British 64's, but for the rest he had to rely on four 56's and one obsolete two-decked 44-gun ship. Above all, in this brisk wind and high sea, the British experience in seamanship and heavy weather gunnery, while his own ships had been confined to harbour and his own gun drills had taken place on smooth water, must tell. The British had one other decisive advantage in close action; this was the number of carronades their ships mounted on the forecastle and quarter-deck – short, wide-barrelled pieces throwing a devastating weight of grape or round shot which equalled that from the great lower-deck guns of first-rates. De Winter's ships only had light guns above the main deck – no carronades whatever.

The action began soon after twelve o'clock, when Rear-Admiral Reyntjes' *Jupiter* opened at the *Monarch* bearing down close upon her; like the British, the Dutch were in the habit of holding their fire, not wasting it outside effective range, and they aimed at the hull. Onslow held on in silence with immense resolution through the hail of shot, steering for a gap in the line just astern of the Dutch flagship, which he shortly passed through; at the same time he opened both broadsides to rake the *Haarlem* – astern of the *Jupiter* –

and the flagship herself. Meanwhile a Dutch 44-gun frigate, the
Monnikendam, Captain-Lieutenant Lancaster, had sailed bravely
into position to block the gap just to leeward of the line proper; as
the *Monarch* rounded up to surge under the lee of the *Jupiter* her
starboard guns swept Lancaster's frigate at short range, wrecking
her wheel, cutting her rigging so that she fell off downwind. Close
on the *Monarch*'s quarter, the *Powerful* broke through the same gap
in the line, again raking the *Haarlem* with her starboard battery,
and carrying on, opened her bow guns on the *Monnikendam* as she
fell off – almost completing her destruction. At the same time the
100   *Montagu* closed on the 56-gun ship following the *Haarlem* and

the *Russell* fell upon the rear 56-gun ship; astern of them came the *Director* and the *Monmouth*, the latter passing through between the two rear 56's, while the *Director* engaged them from the windward berth, soon passing up the line to engage the *Haarlem*, already under the *Powerful*'s fire from the lee berth. 'The rest of the division came on and on all sides there was general firing. The Dutch gave way and the ships became mixed, so that it required sometimes great caution to prevent firing into one another.'

While the Dutch rear maintained this hopelessly unequal combat with great courage in heavy rain squalls, the *Venerable* drew up towards Admiral De Winter's flagship, *Vrijheid*. Winter's next

The British van breaks through the Dutch line.

101

astern, the 74-gun *Staten General*, Rear-Admiral Storij, was second-ing her ably; he had closed until his jibboom almost touched the flagship's taffrail, and as the *Venerable* bore down both Dutch 74's opened their broadsides into her bows. Duncan, seeing that it was impossible to break between them, ordered his helm over and swung to starboard towards the gap that had opened astern of the *Staten General*, shortly passing through – when the Venerables rose, roaring huzzas, discharging their larboard broadside into that ship's stern with devastating effect. They gave her a second broad-side while rounding up in her lee, and she fell off in some confusion. Meanwhile the *Ardent*, 64, which had been close on the *Venerable*'s larboard quarter, fetched up alongside De Winter's flagship, and was soon suffering from her well-aimed fire, reinforced some fifteen minutes later with the fire of the 68-gun ship seconding her ahead. Within ten minutes the *Ardent*'s captain had fallen, mortally wounded, and the cockpit filled with injured, many dreadfully mangled. The *Venerable* brought some relief by engaging the *Vrij-heid* on her lee quarter. But as the unmarked Dutch ships in the centre, together with a Dutch frigate, sailed up and joined the close mêlée, the two British found themselves surrounded and in danger of being overwhelmed; the two other 74's and the smaller ships of Duncan's division had sailed up to the Dutch van, or held off to windward. Duncan, like Howe, had hoisted numeral '5' with red bunting above, 'Engage the enemy closer', long since, but like Howe's some of his captains disappointed.

By now De Winter's orderly line was no more; there were only confused mêlées at what had been van and rear, and ships from what had been the centre either sailing into the cluster around the commanders-in-chief, or passing to leeward, joined by the second ship in the van which had fallen downwind with her captain dying. To add to the confusion, a shot from one of Duncan's 74's had ignited powder under the poop bulwarks of the Dutch *Hercules*, two ships ahead of the *Vrijheid*; flames leaped up the rigging, her sails caught fire and she drifted downwind into the mêlée about the flagships, forcing all captains to make way lest she light their ships. She had ceased firing and her guns' crews were passing up cart-ridges and hurling them into the sea. The diversion provided a respite for the hard-pressed *Venerable* and *Ardent*. Meanwhile, some of the surplus ships from Onslow's lee division, having overwhelmed the Dutch rear and forced all four ships of the line and the frigate, *Monnikendam*, to strike between one o'clock and 1.45, had set fore and mainsails and stood up to engage the Dutch supporting De Winter, turning this crisis point of the battle decisively in Duncan's favour.

Two of these ships, the 74-gun *Powerful* and the relatively little damaged 64, *Director*, engaged De Winter's flagship, which had already suffered severely from the *Venerable* and *Ardent*. Although her guns' crews put up a dour resistance for another hour and De Winter, the sole officer unscathed on the upper deck, refused to haul down the colours, by three o'clock she was a beaten ship. The *Director* closed to within twenty yards of her larboard quarter and poured in shot, then ranged up and lay off her bows, raking her again and again until all her masts came down. Their tangled wreckage lay over the starboard side, masking the guns, whereupon the *Director* lay herself alongside and hailed, asking if she had struck. 'What do you think about it?' was the enigmatic reply. De Winter, who had had been trying to hoist signals for assistance himself, but had the halyards and then the masts themselves shot away, sent for a carpenter to repair a small punt in which he hoped to transfer his flag to another ship. He was kneeling beside the boat holding a square of lead over a shot hole in the timbers while the carpenter hammered a nail in when he was found by the boarding party. 'This my destiny not foreseen,' he said quietly. After making his farewells to a desperately wounded young officer who lay among the wreckage on the quarterdeck, he preceded the British lieutenant to the entrance port and climbed down into the waiting boat below. He was rowed to the *Venerable*, where he took his sword and held it out to Duncan. Duncan refused it, thrusting out his hand instead. 'I would much rather take a brave man's hand than his sword.'

A few days afterwards he described De Winter:

a most agreeable man he is. I have assured him, and with justice, that nothing could exceed his gallantry. He says nothing hurts him but he is the first Dutch admiral ever surrendered. So much more credit to me. I believe the pilot and myself were the only two unhurt on the quarter-deck, and De Winter, who is tall and big as I am, was the only one on his quarterdeck left alive.

De Winter remarked, 'It is a matter of marvel that two such gigantic objects as Admiral Duncan and myself should have escaped the general carnage of this day.'

With De Winter's flagship in ruins and under tow and four others of the Dutch van, together with another frigate, also captured, those Dutch ships which had been supporting the *Vrijheid* retired towards the coast. Duncan could not chase; already he was sounding nine fathoms, and with several of his ships badly damaged, both in masts and in the lower hulls, with the dark October day drawing to a close, his whole attention was directed to keeping his fleet off the coast. Firing ceased.

Admiral Duncan refuses
Admiral de Winter's
proffered sword aboard
the *Venerable* at Camperdown; 'I would much
rather take a brave
man's hand than his
sword'.

In the cockpits and dim orlop decks of the most battered ships, the surgeons and their assistants, already exhausted, smeared with gore from head to foot, continued to select the severely wounded from amongst the scores seeking attention, 'cheered the patient fortitude of others, and sometimes extorted a smile of satisfaction from the mangled sufferers, and succeeded to throw gleams of cheerfulness among so many horrors'. The casualties were heaviest on the two Dutch flagships; both had almost half their complement of some 550 men killed or wounded, a staggering loss, and testimony to heroic resistance. The two British flagships which had taken their first fire before breaking the line had also suffered heavily, but not in the same proportion; the *Monarch* had thirty-six killed, one hundred wounded out of nearly six hundred men, the *Venerable* fifteen killed, sixty-two wounded. Of all the British ships, the hardest hit was the 64-gun *Ardent* which had taken on De Winter's flagship. Aloft she was a wreck with her mizen mast, fore yards, spritsail yards, jibboom and all her running rigging shot away so that she was unmanageable and had to be taken in tow; from her complement of under five hundred, forty-one had been killed and 107 wounded; they had been brought down in such numbers during the action that after filling the wing berths and the accessible parts of the deck forward of the cockpit, they had to be laid on top of each other at the foot of the ladder. The ship's surgeon, Robert Young, asked for another surgeon to be sent over to assist him after the fighting had stopped, but even so he worked without rest until four o'clock the following morning, wondering towards the end whether he would be able to complete each operation he started or whether he would drop from fatigue.

'Melancholy cries for assistance were addressed to me from every side by wounded and dying, and piteous moans and bewailing from pain and despair. In the midst of these agonising scenes I was able to preserve myself firm and collected.'

Many of the worst wounded were stoical beyond belief; they were determined not to flinch and, when news of the shattering victory was brought down to them, they raised a cheer and 'declared they regretted not the loss of their limbs'.

On board the flagship Duncan assembled all his men that were able to come on deck and had the chaplain 'return thanks to Almighty God for all His mercies showered on them and him'. That night, while his fleet and the wrecked and dismasted prizes in tow worked offshore, while carpenters' gangs made the rounds of the lower and orlop decks, plugging shot holes where the sea surged in, shoring up shattered timbers, knees and beams, while the able-bodied cleared the decks of the wreckage and grisly remains of battle, consigned the dead to the sea, worked the pumps continuously, knotted or spliced the broken rigging, rove new halyards, sent up fresh spars, while the surgeons and their mates and assistants worked in a haze of fatigue and foul air way below, Duncan never closed his eyes; his thoughts tossed in the turmoil through which he had just passed; overriding all his 'most constant reflection was a profound thankfulness to God'.

The result of the action was to erase the Dutch fleet as a significant factor in the naval combination against England; of the sixteen two-decked ships De Winter had taken to sea, no less than nine were captured, two of them 74-gun ships and another five mounting between 64 and 68 guns each; in addition two heavy frigates had been taken. As it turned out all were too shattered to be of any use in the Royal Navy, indeed one sank under tow on the way to Yarmouth, but their loss to the Dutch released a number of heavy ships from home fleets for other duties. Two years later a

British force captured the island of Texel, together with Helder Point on the mainland opposite, and the small remaining Dutch fleet surrendered without a shot.

The moral effect of Camperdown was as significant as the strategic; coming in 'the year of the mutinies' it was seen as a heroic atonement, especially as seven of the ships taking part had been amongst those which had refused to accompany Duncan to the Dutch coast earlier, and two of these, *Ardent* and *Belliqueux*, had taken the worst punishment in the mêlée at the head of the line. Above all, despite the British edge in size of ships and guns, the unprecedented scale of the victory, nine out of sixteen, was added proof of the overwhelming dominance of the Royal Navy over all other fleets.

> Monsieurs, Mynheers and Dons, your country's empty boast,
> Our tars can beat all three, each on his native coast.

Duncan actually believed that the battle would have been an annihilation had he met De Winter further from the coast: 'We were obliged, from being so near the land, to be rather rash in our attack. Had we been ten leagues at sea none would have escaped.'

Tactically the battle held fascinating lessons: it seemed to show that Howe's tactic of cutting through the line was feasible even against steady gunners who husbanded their fire until within close range and aimed for the hull in the British style. Perhaps it also advanced Howe's tactic of breaking through in line of bearing; unwittingly, simply because of the need for haste before De Winter reached shoal water, Duncan's attack had been made in two massed groups, almost columns with wide fronts which had overwhelmed the smaller numbers of ships in the parts of the line they broke. Equally unplanned, as it had depended on the positions of the Dutch flagships, had been the concentrations on rear and van, leaving the centre unattacked; this idea had been expounded by one of the earliest of the French tacticians, and incorporated in Howe's own code of tactics. Against the advantages of these well-placed concentrations as they (fortuitously) developed were the difficulties of firing at the enemy without endangering friends, and the heavy casualties among those ships which took the first shock of the close fighting. Not more than ten out of the sixteen were involved in the close work, although only one captain was actually dismissed the service for cowardice. The Dutch suffered severely with some 1,160 killed or wounded, but the British total of 825 casualties was far more than they had come to expect, and of those nearly seven hundred came from only seven ships, *Venerable*,

Monarch, *Ardent*, *Belliqueux*, *Powerful*, *Triumph* and *Bedford*. For Howe, and probably for Duncan himself, the disadvantages of such an irregular attack as a general rule outweighed the advantages. As Howe put it:

> The chief purposes for which a fleet is formed in line of battle are: that the ships may be able to assist and support each other in action; that they may not be exposed to the fire of the enemy's ships greater in number than themselves; that every ship may be able to fire on the enemy without risk of firing into the ships of her own fleet.

Such was the old school of tactics. But did the extraordinary advantages of Duncan's pell-mell attack, both in theory and in the decisive result achieved, cause the recently appointed Rear-Admiral Horatio Nelson to ponder?

The jubilation in England and Scotland (especially) when the North Sea Fleet returned to Yarmouth with its shattered prizes was almost past expression. 'What shall I say to you my dear and victorious Admiral?' wrote Lady Spencer, the First Lord's wife, to Duncan:

> Where shall I find words to convey to you the slightest idea of the enthusiasm created by your glorious, splendid and memorable achievements? Not in the English language; and no other is worthy of being used upon so truly British an exploit. The man who has struggled thro' all the difficulties of everlasting North Sea cruises, of hardships of every kind, of storms, of cold, of perpetual disappointments, without a murmur, without a regret, and lastly who most unprecedently braved an enemy's fleet of 16 or 20 sail of the line with only two Men of War in a state of mutiny to oppose them: *That Man*, acquiring the honour and glory you have done on the 11th of October did not surprise me.

Chapter 4

The Nile

While the scarred figurehead of the *Vrijheid* was towed to Scotland to adorn the estate of 'Viscount Duncan of Camperdown', and public subscriptions, soon topping £50,000, were opened for the relief of the families of those killed and wounded in the battle, Nelson was convalescing in Bath after having his right arm amputated. The elbow had been shattered by grapeshot while he had led an assault on the Spanish port of Santa Cruz in the Canary Islands that summer. He still felt excruciating pain at times in the short stump; a nerve had been caught up in one of the ligatures binding the arteries. Worse than extreme physical pain had been the blow to his self-esteem; the assault had failed ignominiously. After the acclaim and supremely gratifying public recognition of his exploits at St Vincent, the failure had tumbled him into black depression.

It had not affected the high opinion of him held by Jervis, now Earl of St Vincent. That winter, as he recovered his spirits and the ligature was at last expelled from his stump and the pains ceased, his requests to return to duty were warmly welcomed. In April 1798 he sailed in the 74-gun *Vanguard* to rejoin the old admiral who was still off Cadiz blockading the Spanish force he had defeated the previous year. St Vincent was delighted; 'The arrival of Admiral Nelson has given me new life,' he wrote to the First Lord on 1 May. He had a special reason: reports had been coming in for some months of a considerable expedition being prepared at Toulon under the command of General Bonaparte, with transports assembling at Marseilles and Genoa, whose destination was obscure – 'according to some reports Sicily or Corfu, and according to others Portugal or Ireland'. It was necessary to send a squadron through the straits to watch the activity and shadow the force when it emerged. Nelson was the ideal choice for such a delicate independent command and he had no sooner arrived than St Vincent sent him with two other 74's and two frigates into the Mediterranean 'to endeavour to ascertain the real object of the preparations making by the French'.

The Admiralty was even more anxious about Bonaparte's preparations, and at about the same time despatched eight sail of the line from the Channel Fleet to St Vincent, instructing him to send a squadron of twelve of the line off Toulon. Spencer himself was so impressed by the awful possibilities that in an accompanying letter he described a new British naval presence in the Mediterranean as 'a condition on which the fate of Europe at this moment may be stated to depend'. Every hazard was to be incurred in effecting it.

Nelson in his prime.

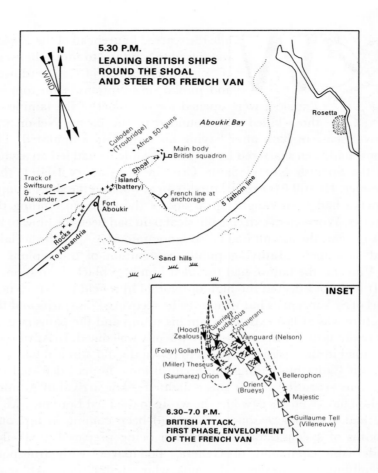

5.30 P.M.
**LEADING BRITISH SHIPS
ROUND THE SHOAL
AND STEER FOR FRENCH VAN**

N

WIND

Aboukir Bay

Rosetta

Culloden
(Troubridge)
Africa 50-guns

Main body
British squadron

Track of
Swiftsure
&
Alexander

Shoal

Island
(battery)

French line at
anchorage

5 fathom line

Fort
Aboukir

Rocks

To Alexandria

Sand hills

INSET

(Hood)
Zealous

Guerrier

Audacious

Conquerant

Vanguard (Nelson)

(Foley) Goliath

(Miller) Theseus

(Saumarez) Orion

Bellerophon

Orient
(Brueys)

Majestic

Guillaume Tell
(Villeneuve)

6.30–7.0 P.M.
**BRITISH ATTACK,
FIRST PHASE, ENVELOPMENT
OF THE FRENCH VAN**

Map 5
Opening of the Battle of
the Nile, 1 August 1798.

And for the commander he suggested Nelson, 'whose acquaintance with that part of the world, as well as his activity and disposition seem to qualify him in a peculiar manner for the service'.

St Vincent decided to send Nelson, already off Toulon, ten of the 'choice' ships which formed his advanced or inshore squadron off Cadiz. He placed them under the orders of his favourite captain, Thomas Troubridge, and as the sails of his own reinforcements appeared above the horizon on 23 May, ordered Troubridge to prepare to sail. As soon as it was dark the inshore squadron set course for the Straits of Gibraltar; before daylight the next morning another squadron had taken its place, 'parading under the walls of Cadiz'.

Nelson meanwhile had been forced off station by a gale which came near to destroying the *Vanguard* and all aboard her. His captain, Berry, described it:

Before 12 at night the gale came on, and increased with rapid violence, which obliged us to furl all sails and try under a main storm staysail. At about two the main topmast went over the side with the topsail yard full of men; fortunately only one man fell overboard and one fell on the booms and was killed on the spot. At half past two the mizen topmast went over the side; the foremast gave an alarming crack, and at quarter past three went by the board with a most tremendous crash, and what was very extraordinary it fell in two pieces across the forecastle. Our situation was really alarming; the wreck of the fore topmast and foremast hanging over the side and beating against the ship's bottom: the best bower anchor was flung out of its place and was also thumping the bottom; the wreck of the main topmast swinging violently against the main rigging, every roll endangering the loss of the mainmast, which we expected to fall every moment ... and knowing we were driving on an enemy's shore.

By using a tattered fragment of the spritsail still left, and watching for a lull in the seas, Berry managed to get her around on the

Orion (Captain Sir James Saumarez) comes to anchor with the rest of the choice 'inshore squadron' blockading the Spanish fleet in Cadiz, which can be seen behind.

Thomas Troubridge,
whom St Vincent
thought the finest
officer in the Service,
as a Rear-Admiral after
the Battle of the Nile.

other tack, and after thirty-six strenuous hours during which the almost dismasted ship laboured heavily and shipped dangerous quantities of water, the gale eased sufficiently to allow one of the other 74's, the *Alexander*, to take her in tow. Hardly had this been accomplished than the wind dropped away practically to nothing and the ships found themselves embayed off the south-west of Sardinia, drifting helplessly shorewards. Nelson ordered the *Alexander*'s captain, Alexander Ball, to cast off and save his own vessel, but Ball refused. And at the last moment a wind sprang up allowing the *Vanguard* to be towed out, just weathering a fringe of rocks.

'I ought not to call what has happened to the *Vanguard* by the cold name of accident,' Nelson wrote to his wife. 'I believe, firmly, that it was the Almighty's goodness to check my consummate vanity. I hope it has made me a better officer as I feel confident it has made me a better Man.'

When, after four days at anchor, the *Vanguard* had been fitted with a slender jury foremast, topmasts and yards, the little squadron returned off Toulon only to find the great expedition had sailed in their absence – who knew where? – and that the British frigates,

Edward Berry, Captain
of Nelson's flagship at
the Battle of the Nile.

expecting that the *Vanguard* must have run for the dockyard at
Gibraltar, had made there themselves. However, Troubridge's
ten of the line joined shortly and, suspecting that the French
purpose was an assault on the Dual Monarchy of Naples and
Sicily, Nelson immediately steered east, making Ischia off the
Neapolitan coast on 15 June. Troubridge was sent in to see the
British Ambassador, Sir William Hamilton, and the Prime Minister – also English – Sir John Acton, to gain intelligence and ask
for naval reinforcements, particularly frigates without which the
squadron was largely blind. However, the kingdom was at peace
and could not help without compromising its neutrality and inviting French assault; Troubridge could get no more than a promise
that if the kingdom were attacked its whole naval force would be
placed under Nelson's command. He did, however, learn that the
French had attacked Malta the week before. At once Nelson set
sail to pass through the Straits of Messina, writing to Sir William
Hamilton as he went to remind him of Naples' unique opportunity
to win a share in the glory of destroying the French 'pests of the
human race'. He ended by paying his best respects to Lady Hamil-   113

ton; he had met her once five years before while trying to obtain Neapolitan troops to help Lord Hood defend Toulon, and had not forgotten; it was difficult to forget the most scintillating jewel at the court. 'Tell her I hope to be presented to her crowned with laurel or cyprus ...'

Arriving off Messina on the 20th, he learnt that Malta had fallen to the French, the Knights of St John having given up their ancient possessions and accumulated treasure with scant resistance. Two days later off the extreme southern cape of Sicily he spoke to a brig out of Malta and learnt that Bonaparte had sailed from there on the 16th with sixteen of the line, frigates, mortar vessels, gunboats and some three hundred transports filled with troops; he had given out his destination as Sicily. As Nelson had run down the whole east coast of Sicily without gaining any indication of a French attempt on the island, and as the winds had been westerly for several days, he became convinced that Bonaparte's real destination was Egypt. The suspicion had been forming for some time. Before reaching Ischia he had written to the First Lord, 'If they pass Sicily I shall believe they are going on their scheme of possessing Alexandria, and getting more troops to India – a plan concerted with Tippoo Sahib, by no means so difficult as might at first be imagined.' Now, after a council with his most trusted captains, he crowded sail directly for Alexandria, writing to the British consul there, 'I think their object is to possess themselves of some port in Egypt, and to fix themselves at the head of the Red Sea, in order to get a formidable army into India, and in concert with Tippoo Sahib, to drive us if possible, from India.'

114

Nelson's prime object as the squadron drove easterly with a fresh wind from astern, was to destroy Bonaparte's transports, containing as he thought 40,000 troops, field artillery, cavalry and engineers' supply train. His plans had been prepared and explained to all his captains soon after Troubridge's force had joined; if they met the enemy at sea the squadron was to divide into three parts, one of five ships led by the *Vanguard* and one of four ships were to attack and contain the French sixteen of the line; the third division of four ships was to concern itself solely with the destruction of the fleet of transports. The details of different forms of attack according to the enemy dispositions and the state of the wind were thrashed out with all the captains in numerous meetings aboard the *Vanguard* whenever the weather permitted, so that all knew Nelson's intentions and would be able to act on their own initiative in accord with the spirit of the plans whatever unforeseen contingencies might arise. The same detailed attention was given to the possibility of meeting the enemy at anchor; the central idea of all the schemes for attack was to throw overwhelming concentrations on parts of the line, subduing these before the rest of the ships could come to their aid. In taking all the captains into his confidence, making certain that they understood the grand principles, above all in unaffectedly placing his trust in *them*, creating an inspired 'band of brothers', Nelson differed from his great predecessors. He differed too in his conception of naval war. He looked not for victory in the old style, a few prizes taken, the enemy forced back into their ports, but *annihilation*. 'Now had we taken ten sail and allowed the eleventh to escape, when it had been possible to have got at her,' he had written after one of the frustrating partial engagements in the Mediterranean three years before, 'I could never have called it well done.'

He hated the French with all his ardent nature – for their atheism, their attempts to overthrow all established order, for the atrocities they had committed against their own people and their armies had committed through Europe; 'he had such a horror of all Frenchmen', one close observer wrote, 'that I believe he thought them nearly as corrupt in body as in mind.' And when he fought them, he did so on behalf of the great God he worshipped. Believing too in the unequalled skill, courage and fighting ability of his men, eager for the artistic and intellectual satisfaction of using them as he knew they could be used, decisively, impatient for the world to ring again with his own name and qualities, thirsting renown above others, he brought altogether new dimensions to naval war.

As the squadron paced easterly on a direct course for Alexandria it passed by the lumbering mass of the French transports out of sight after dark and, pressing on, arrived off the port on the 28th. All was quiet. There was no hint of the French anywhere in Egypt. Worried that he had taken the wrong decision, that Bonaparte had after all been making for Sicily – or was he simply watering his armada at Corfu? – Nelson set off again to search northerly on a north-west wind, writing a lament to St Vincent about his lack of frigates, 'to which I shall ever attribute my ignorance of the situation of the French fleet'.

His first guess had been right. Bonaparte was making for Egypt. He had put the idea to the Directorate the previous year after his successes had forced Austria out of the war. A French colony in Egypt, he had suggested, would compensate for their losses to the British in the West Indies and the Cape of Good Hope and serve as a springboard to cut British trade and possessions in the Red Sea and India. These were rationalisations for his own ambition; throughout history, he believed, all great glory had been won in the East; he would emulate the conquests of Alexander the Great. The Directorate had suggested that he should strike instead at the *heart* of the chief enemy – invade England, march on London where all the misfortunes of Europe were planned and paid for. But Bonaparte's thoughts had been fixed on the East. After ordering flotillas of small craft to carry an 'Army of England' he had pointed to the impossibility of convoying them safely across unless the French fleet had command in the Channel, and had continued to press his own scheme. The Directorate, quite willing by now to have such a dangerously popular and ambitious general occupied as far east as he cared to go, soon agreed to his grand conception, gave him more troops than he asked for and even supported his idea to combine the conquest of Egypt with a scientific expedition to rediscover its lost civilizations; archaeologists, artists, astronomers, mineralogists, surveyors, engineers, leading names in the sciences were enlisted, together with administrators for the new colony of Egypt, all in the most astonishing secrecy. Thirteen ships of the line were provided as a battle fleet to cover the huge expedition and put under Vice-Admiral Brueys d'Aigalliers, an experienced but remarkably indecisive officer of the old Royalist Navy, who was to fly his flag in the first-rate *Orient* of 120 guns. Such was the force that Nelson narrowly missed on passage to Alexandria, and would have seen following him in had he waited two days.

Bonaparte lost no time in occupying Alexandria and the smaller Delta towns, and with his transports safely moored in the old port, marched inland for Cairo, which he entered on 22 July. As he

Opposite Admiral Brueys d'Aigalliers, whose fleet was not sufficiently prepared to meet Nelson's inspired assault.

116

poured all his great energy into winning over influential sections of the Egyptian population and setting up the administrative machinery for his new French colony, Nelson, who had made a rapid sweep around the north-eastern part of the Mediterranean, was back in Sicily at the port of Syracuse taking on fresh provisions – twenty live bullocks each ship and plentiful supplies of lemons and onions. Hearing no more of the French, on 24 July he sailed easterly again for the Greek islands, where, at last, he picked up certain information that Bonaparte had attacked Egypt; once again he crowded sail direct for Alexandria.

Three days later, on 1 August, on a fine clear morning with a pleasant north-north-westerly breeze on the quarter, the great pharos of the old city rose from the south-eastern horizon some twenty-four miles away. Shortly after noon the *Alexander* and *Swiftsure*, which Nelson had sent on ahead of the squadron, made out from the forest of masts in both old and new ports two French ships of the line and six frigates; French colours flew from scores of merchant ships and from the towers of the castles. The *Alexander* made the signal 'Enemy in sight'. But it was not the main battle fleet which, now Bonaparte was ashore, formed the prime target. One and a half hours later as the squadron pressed on in no regular order lookouts aloft on the royal yards of the two most easterly ships, *Zealous* and *Goliath*, sighted masts above the land some way to the east of the city in Aboukir Bay; scanned with a glass they proved to be ships of the line. The midshipman of the *Goliath*, anxious that his ship should have the honour of signalling the enemy battle fleet first, slid down the backstay to report instead of alerting the *Zealous* by calling to the deck, but it was the *Zealous* which broke the signal first. Some twenty minutes later when the number of battleships at Aboukir had been reported as sixteen – as it turned out there were only thirteen and four frigates – Nelson ordered the squadron to come to the wind on the larboard tack and shaped course for the Bay. It was nearly three o'clock; the *Alexander* and *Swiftsure*, some nine miles south of the main body, were recalled, and Troubridge in the *Culloden*, some distance astern with a captured wine brig in tow, was ordered to cast off his prize.

By four o'clock the *Vanguard* had opened the bay sufficiently to see, past Fort Aboukir at the north-western extremity of the low sand spit which shelved into the calm blue expanse of water, all thirteen French sail of the line anchored in compact order of battle heading about north-north-west; they were close in to the western shore with frigates and gunboats inside. Nelson assumed that

118 Brueys would have placed both head and tail of his line close in to

shoal water; nevertheless, where there was water for a French ship to swing there must be water for a British to anchor alongside. At 4.20 he made the general signal to prepare for battle, and to prepare for anchoring with cables from the stern ports, and half an hour later to attack the enemy's van and centre. His intentions were now clear to all his captains without further signals; from their frequent discussions about just such a situation, they knew what was required. With the wind blowing almost straight down the French line from van to rear they would fall on the leading ships, one British vessel on the bow, one on the quarter of each Frenchman, and pound them into silence before the rear ships could work up against the wind to support them. Afterwards they could destroy the rear. In essence it was simple; in practice it would need skills of a high order for they had no charts of the bay and there was a shoal extending north-easterly from the end of the land which they would need to round before they could get to the head of the line; there were also the French broadsides as they ran down, and there was the evening which would be upon them while some of the ships were still working around the shoals.

'I knew what stuff I had under me,' Nelson explained afterwards. 'Had I taken a fleet of the same force straight from Spithead I would sooner have thought of flying than attacking the French in their position.' His mind was prepared by constant pre-thinking, he knew his captains and seizing immediately on the fatal flaw in the French position – being Nelson – he knew there was no time to be lost. The plan mirrored his own qualities, boldness, spontaneous recognition of the essentials in the situation, impatience of delay, spirit, flair.

Directly his mind was made up his spirits rose. During the long chase he had been increasingly fretful and had hardly slept or eaten, wondering whether his assumptions about the French had been wrong. Now, while his quarters were knocked down by the carpenters' gangs and his furniture was carried to the main hatch and swung below, he invited his officers to dine, discussing the chances of the evening with the eager liveliness he invariably showed at the prospect of action. As they rose to go to their stations, he exclaimed, 'Before this time tomorrow I shall have gained a peerage or Westminster Abbey!'

Lookouts in the French fleet had sighted Nelson's topsails about the same time as their own masts had been reported by the *Zealous*. Brueys, knowing that a British squadron was in the area, had given orders for parties of men working ashore to return to their ships, and an hour later, sure that it was his enemy now steering towards

Two of the 'Band of Brothers' in later years: left, Samuel Hood of the *Zealous*; right, Sir James Saumarez of the *Orion*.

the bay with a crowd of canvas, had ordered the ships cleared for action. He had not believed they would attack so late in the afternoon and in such ragged and extended order as they were, but as the leading group began to wear around the end of the shoal and, coming before the wind, set studding sails, he realised suddenly that he would have to fight before nightfall.

Ever since taking up his position in the bay early in July he had been undecided whether to give battle at anchor or in the open sea if the enemy should come; he was still undecided. The bay was too open to make the position impregnable, although he had made some attempts to strengthen it by constructing a battery – half-heartedly – on a low island which rose from the shoal to the north-

120

east of Fort Aboukir, and had placed his weakest and oldest ships at the van close in to the shoaling water a mile or so below the island. The rest of the ships he had anchored at intervals of 250 feet one from another in a shallow bow curving in to shoal water at the tail of the line. The strongest point was in the centre, where he had placed his own 120-gun flagship, *Orient*, seconded ahead and astern by powerful 80-gun two-deckers. Astern of this group were two 74's, then another 80-gun ship, *Guillaume Tell*, flying the flag of Rear-Admiral Villeneuve, who commanded his rear division – and finally two 74's. He expected any attacking fleet to be deterred by the shoal and his shore battery at the head of the line and to fall on the centre and rear, even perhaps to promenade outside the line from the rear.

As the leading British entered the bay and steered for the van instead his first impression was that he should weigh and fight under sail, and he had his t'gallant yards swayed aloft. Almost immediately the disadvantages of trying to work out of the bay and fight at the same time with his ill-trained crews came home to him, and he made a signal that he intended to fight at anchor. Each ship was to let go a second anchor, also to send a cable to her next astern with a hawser bent on to it some one hundred feet along its length and taken to the opposite side so that it could be used to heave the ship into directions where the broadside would bear. Some ships obeyed, most failed.

The leading British ships were the *Goliath* (Captain Foley), *Zealous* (Captain Hood), and the *Vanguard*. They had been more or less abreast of each other while standing easterly past the shoal, the *Vanguard* slightly back on the weather quarter of the *Zealous*; Nelson had called out to ask Hood whether he thought they were far enough to the eastward to bear up round the shoal. 'I cannot say,' Hood had replied. 'We have eleven fathoms of water – but if you will allow me the honour of leading into battle, I will keep the lead going and lead you as close as I can. It appears to shoal regularly.'

'You have my leave,' Nelson had replied, and wishing him success, swept off his hat. Hood, in replying to the flourish, let his own hat slip over the side. 'Never mind,' he said, turning to his first lieutenant. 'There it goes for luck! Put the helm up and make sail!' Thomas Foley, close to leeward, had anticipated the movement, and put his helm up and hoisted his studding sails at the same time; having the inside berth he edged into the lead instead of Hood. It was nearly 5.30 by then; the sun was low over the western horizon.

The *Vanguard* shortly hoisted a signal for the ships following to alter course to starboard as convenient, then backed her topsails and hove-to in order to speak to the brig *Mutine* – the sole small craft with the squadron – which had taken some local sailors from a vessel out of Alexandria to help as pilots. The ship next astern, *Theseus*, Captain Miller, went past; in passing she was hailed by the flagship to be the admiral's second ahead, so hove-to near by, and presently the *Orion* and *Audacious* sailed up to take third and fourth positions in the line. There was a long gap between them and the two leaders, who were still carrying all sail, taking continuous soundings as they leaned in towards shoal water near the head of the enemy – white topsails and t'gallants against blue sky, black and yellow hulls chequered with the red of raised port lids, the dull muzzles of cannon protruding in a double line to the gilded stern-walks, they stood on in stately and awful silence, broken only by the rising and falling cadences of the leadsman in the chains. Ahead of them the enemy masts and rigging stood sharp in the clear light; beyond, the low sand shore rose from greening water, its bright upper edge honed like a desert sword. Hidden within the picture in the endless quiet ten thousand French and British men and youths, frowning with concentration, screwed down their nerves – ten thousand urgent private images hung suspended before the act.

Suddenly at 6.15 the French ships, some of which had been heaving on the hawsers to open their broadsides across the course of the British, hoisted their colours; as the *Goliath* closed inside five hundred yards, shortening sail as the soundings approached the danger mark of five fathoms, the second French, *Conquérant*, opened fire; the thunder spread up and down the line until all ahead of the great three-decker, *Orient*, were wreathed in smoke, and at the same time the smaller guns and mortars on the island battery opened from the other side. As was usual, most of the French shot went high; the balls zipped and cracked through the British rigging, now bare of canvas below the topsails. The British guns' crews remained silent. The ships pressed through the perfectly calm water now tinged pink from a fiery western sky as the sun neared the horizon.

In the starboard chains of the *Goliath* the leadsman called his descending scale: 'By the deep, six – a quarter less six ...' Thomas Foley, listening intently from the forward rail of the quarterdeck, estimated the distance to the bowsprit and jibboom poking from the smoke clouding the broadside of the leading Frenchman, *Guerrière*. 'I should like to get inside her,' he said to the Master. 'I shouldn't be surprised to find him unprepared on the inner side.' 123

Foley was a huge, even-natured man; that penetrating judge, St Vincent, had found behind his blue eye and heavy look 'a sound and excellent understanding, great temper and a pleasant wit'. He had talked before of surprising an anchored enemy by leading in between him and the land and attacking his perhaps unready side. Now he had the opportunity. The danger of fetching up hard on the shoaling botton before he reached the *Guerrière* was real, but seeing her anchor buoy at the usual distance some two hundred yards ahead of her, he determined to attempt a passage between the buoy and the end of her jibboom, and sent the Master forward with instructions to let go the anchor directly they were one ship's length inside the Frenchman.

'And a quarter, five – by the mark, five – by the mark, five …'

As he approached within two hundred yards of the *Guerrière* Foley gave the order to open fire when the guns bore. The order was repeated by the officers of the quarters between decks; tension broke; three full-throated cheers swept raggedly across the bay, answered by the men of the *Zealous* astern. The foremost guns, angled to their extreme forward bearing, crashed out in groups double- and sometimes treble-shotted; the first splintered holes opened through the French bow timbers. In the dense smoke blown down towards the *Guerrière*, the *Goliath* swept past her jibboom, raking her from end to end with another broadside, then wore round to parallel her inside. The Master gave orders to cut away the anchor, whose cable had been led out through a gunroom port at the stern and forward again outside everything to the cathead. But the lashings proved obstinate and the ship was almost abreast of the Frenchman before the anchor splashed into the water. As Foley had guessed, her larboard guns were not even run out and bags and boxes could be seen obstructing the upper-deck ports. They gave her another broadside as they ran on, veering the cable until they eventually brought up abreast the second in the line, *Conquérant*, an old vessel mounting lighter guns than the others because of her frail timbers. She was equally unprepared as they opened their hot guns against her.

The *Zealous* followed. Hood had not anticipated Foley leading inside and as the soundings fell to five fathoms had expected him to stick fast any moment. But when he went clear, evidently missing his chosen opponent in the van, Hood determined to take his place, steered in his wake, raked as he crossed the *Guerrière*, cut away his anchor moments later and fetched up exactly in position on her inside bow at scarcely more than fifty yards' range, where he opened a terrible fire from double- and treble-shotted guns. Within minutes the timbers between her forward ports were shattered, guns smashed to the deck, foremast, shrouds and stays shot through and through, dead and wounded lying thick, survivors retreating aft out of the zone of splinters and flying wrack. Above, the forecastle and gangways were swept clear of sharpshooters by swathes of grape shot from the British carronades. Within seven minutes from the first raking broadside, her foremast was severed close to the deck and crashed over the side.

The third British ship, *Audacious*, steered between the *Guerrière* and the *Conquérant*, raking and cutting her anchor away as she broke the line, fetching up on the *Conquérant*'s inner bow at about fifty yards. The *Orion* meanwhile diverged to starboard of her wake and followed the *Goliath*'s track across the *Guerrière*'s bows, giving that shattered ship a broadside as she passed, then sweeping in a wide circle around the three engaged British ships; as she did so she was fired on by a large frigate, *Serieuse*, lying inshore of the French line. She replied with one broadside of such terrible effect that the frigate drifted away, filling with water, and hit the sand bottom, whereupon all her masts fell. The *Orion*, briefly going aground herself, finally fetched up to a bow anchor between the fourth and fifth of the French line. Meanwhile the fifth British, *Theseus*, had placed herself inside the third French ship. Her captain, Miller, had been following in the wake of the leaders and had seen the French shot sweeping high.

The British van leads inside the French line anchored in the Bay of Aboukir, and the *Guerrière*, raked by successive ships, loses her foremast.

Knowing well that at such a moment Frenchmen would not have coolness enough to change their elevation, I closed them suddenly, and running under the arch of their shot, reserved my fire until I had the *Guerriere*'s masts in a line and her jibboom about six feet clear of our rigging; we then opened with such terrific effect that a second breath could not be drawn before her main and mizen masts were gone.

The sun was going below the horizon in a blaze of red as the *Theseus* wore smartly, cut between the hulk of the *Guerrière* and the *Zealous*, and after passing within ten feet of the *Goliath* cut away her anchor and brought up abreast of the third Frenchman at about four hundred yards. Nelson, in the meantime, had directed the *Vanguard* to be placed on the outside of the French line; being the sixth ship she shortly fetched up to a stern anchor on the other side of the *Theseus*' opponent. Captain Miller, worried that his shot might hit the *Vanguard*, redirected his forward guns' crews to the fourth Frenchman, his after guns' crews to the second. The next two British ships followed the *Vanguard*'s lead in wearing before they reached the line, and fetched up to stern anchors outside the fourth and fifth French so that the whole enemy van was doubled by an overwhelming concentration.

In the fading light with the smoke of furious cannonading drifting down the French line, the ninth British ship, *Bellerophon*, missed the so-far unengaged sixth Frenchman and attempted to anchor off the bow of the seventh, Brueys' flagship, *Orient*; failing to bring up in

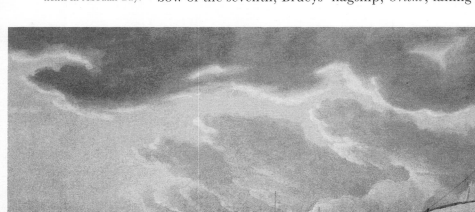

Fire spreads down the line as the British 'double' their opponents in Aboukir Bay.

time she veered abreast of that great ship's broadside and in the fierce duel which developed she began to suffer heavy damage from the three tiers of great guns opposed, and more casualties than the leading British which had run the gauntlet of the first fire from the whole van. After her, one other British 74, *Majestic*, ran in and, anchoring outside the ninth Frenchman, also suffered severely as she was engaged by this ship and the large 80-gun vessel seconding the *Orient* astern.

There were still four British ships not in action. The two which had been sent ahead to reconnoitre Alexandria had been unable to weather the shoal at the entrance to the bay while standing to the eastward, and had had to tack at about the time the leaders wore in to the bay. One small 50-gun ship, lately joined, had been unable to keep up with the 74's, while Troubridge's *Culloden*, some distance astern during the morning because of her tow, had caught up with her and in overtaking to windward had run on to rocks at the extremity of the shoal at the entrance. This was a serious loss; Troubridge's ship was an exceptionally well-trained and effective unit. Despite laying out kedge anchors to heave her off, starting the water and wine in the holds, throwing shot and provisions overboard and loading more into boats – despite the most tremendous exertions she held fast, then her stern began to lift and pound, opening leaks and smashing the rudder off. Troubridge had the inexpressible frustration of being a helpless spectator while the battle rose to a crescendo of noise and pyrotechnics in the dusk; his only consolation was that he acted as a marker for the last two ships rounding the shoal, saving them from his own fate.

By the time they did come into action the French van was in a sorry state. The third ship *Spartiate* was still putting up a heroic resistance to the *Vanguard*, but the ship ahead, totally dismasted, had struck to the *Goliath* after fearful slaughter, and the *Guerrière* was beaten and silent; her captain still refused to accept Hood's repeated calls to submit, so that the *Zealous* was forced to continue firing into the wreck: 'From her bow to her larboard gangway the ports on the maindeck are entirely in one, and her gunwale in that part entirely cut away, two of the main deck beams fallen on the guns in consequence.' Astern of this group the fourth Frenchman was also dismasted and in almost as bad condition, replying only spasmodically to the *Theseus* on her larboard bow and the *Minotaur* outside her, while the fifth French ship had already been beaten out of the line and had drifted down to anchor inshore of the centre. Here the fight was going the other way; the *Orient* had dismasted and wrecked the *Bellerophon* which had cut her cable and

127

was drifting away; the *Majestic*, attacking to astern of the *Orient*, had been caught in a disastrous raking fire when, trying to shift position, her jibboom had become entangled in the main rigging of her opponent.

In this situation the two fresh British ships, *Alexander* and *Swift-sure*, joined shortly by the little 50-gun vessel which had been aiding Troubridge in his unsuccessful attempt to get off the shoal, ran down with sure judgement straight into the centre. Although night had closed down there was a clear moon and the constant gun flashes made it possible to see colours vividly whenever the clouds of smoke permitted; in addition all British ships had hoisted four horizontal lights at the mizen as a distinguishing mark. So the three British captains, perhaps drawn by a huge tricolour flying from the *Orient*'s main, were able to place themselves superbly, one outside the line on the *Orient*'s starboard bow, one on the French flagship's inner quarter, while the 50-gun ship fetched up right across the bows of the *Orient*'s 'second' ahead, and raked her practically un-disturbed. Any shot that missed hit the *Orient*.

As the remaining ships of the French van at last submitted and were taken in possession by boarding parties, the *Orient* and her

'seconds', their crews already depleted, immensely weary from the first wave of the attack, suffered terribly from the new ships. Brueys himself, already wounded in the head and arm, took a round shot in the belly which nearly cut him in two; he asked not to be taken below but to be allowed to die on his own quarterdeck. At about the same time his flag captain was struck in the face by flying wrack and was carried below senseless. Shortly afterwards a fire started in Brueys' cabin. Seeing this the British 74 on the flagship's quarter directed every gun at the flames, creating havoc among the men attempting to extinguish them. Soon the fire had burned through the deckhead to the poop, up the mizen and, helped by jars of oil and paint which had not been stowed below, began to spread uncontrollably through all the decks. The flames lit the bay, the shattered, dismasted ships wreathed in smoke, the confused wreckage, mangled, dismembered, scorched bodies in the water. The heat became intense; men started leaping from the flagship's ports, or scrambling into boats. British captains gave orders for buckets to be hoisted to wet sails and decks in case of flying red-hot splinters when she exploded; some of the nearest veered their cables and fell away; those that remained closed all gun ports. In the

Nelson is treated below decks after being wounded over the eye by a fragment of flying metal at the height of the battle.

Vanguard, the captain went below to tell Nelson, who had been wounded over the eye by flying metal, and escorted him to the deck for a view of the awesome spectacle. Nelson at once gave orders for boats to be sent to rescue survivors.

At ten o'clock the fire reached the French flagship's magazine and she blew apart with a deafening roar; bright, burning wreckage flew over a vast area, scattering red-hot embers over the decks of all nearby ships, friend and foe, and starting numerous fires; guns' crews and magazine parties way below the waterline of the nearest ships felt the blast like a giant's hand shaking the frames and timbers about them. The explosion was followed by a profound silence; many of the embattled guns' crews dropped by their pieces, exhausted, and fell asleep at once. Only the fire parties of the ships which had been nearest the *Orient* were busy extinguishing outbreaks from the burning wreckage which had fallen on them – and the boats' crews which had been sent to rescue those who had leaped into the water. Overhead a thick pall of black smoke obscured the moon.

By now the battle was decided. The *Orient*'s second ahead, now exposed single-handed to several British ships and with some two-

130

thirds of her complement already killed or wounded, had to submit. Those British who had been engaging the *Orient* veered their cables and fell down towards the rear to support the *Majestic*; she, having cleared her bowsprit from the rigging of the ship which had caused her so much destruction earlier, had laid herself athwart the bows of the next astern and was taking a terrible revenge. By midnight the guns' crews of both sides were practically asleep on their feet and fire continued only spasmodically through the small hours; nevertheless two French ships cut their cables and fell to leeward out of range, and the *Orient*'s 'second' astern, completely dismasted, drove ashore.

At dawn the relatively little-damaged British ships from the van got under way and compelled the surrender of most of the remaining ships in the French rear with little trouble. Only two of the line led by Villeneuve and two frigates succeeded in beating out of the bay and making their escape. For all practical purposes the French fleet had been wiped out. As Nelson had longed for, it was victory on a new scale altogether – virtual annihilation. 'Almighty God,' he had started his despatch to St Vincent while the battle still raged in the centre, 'has blessed his Majesty's arms by a great

The *Orient* blows up at the height of the battle.

131

Prayers offered aboard
Nelson's flagship
Vanguard, in thanks-
giving for the British
victory at the Battle of
the Nile.

Victory ...' St Vincent replied when he heard the news, 'My dear
Admiral, God be praised, and you and your gallant band rewarded
by a grateful country for the greatest achievement the history of the
world can produce ...'

Some 1,700 Frenchmen lost their lives in the battle, and rather
under half that number were wounded; the corresponding British
figures were 218 and 677, the worst sufferers being the two ships
which had first engaged the centre, the *Bellerophon* (49 killed, 148
wounded) and *Majestic* (50 killed, 143 wounded); the *Vanguard*,
which had taken the fire of the centre while coming down first into
an outside berth, had lost 30 killed, 75 wounded. By contrast Hood's
Zealous only suffered seven wounded in her engagement in the van.
Of the French prizes, three of the line were so wrecked they were
burnt in the bay, but six of the others were refitted and eventually
commissioned in the Royal Navy. More important than these
material results were the moral and strategic consequences. The
Mediterranean was regained for the Royal Navy, Minorca and
later Malta taken and held as British bases, Bonaparte's army was
cut off from support, Turkey and Egypt encouraged to throw out
the invader, while in Europe the spell of the recent French victories
was broken; Austria and Russia joined a second alliance against
her and the following year drove her armies from the rich north
Italian territories Bonaparte had taken. As for Bonaparte, when
he heard of Turkey's declaration against France, he marched northwards along the coast (through what is now Israel) until held at
Acre, just north of the Bay of Haifa. His failure to take this strategic
point without which he could not risk continuing north was due to

British command at sea. The siege guns with which he could have reduced the ancient fortress in short time were captured while on their way along the coast by sea, and the heroic spirit with which his assaults were thrown back time and again was inspired by Captain – self-styled Commodore – Sir Sydney Smith, who had command of a detached squadron of two 74's in the eastern Mediterranean. Smith, a flamboyant genius with a self-confidence and independence of mind fully equalling Nelson's, later hastened Bonaparte's complete abandonment of the eastern adventure by sending him French newspapers which described the anarchy into which the government of the Republic had fallen. Bonaparte immediately slipped back to France in a frigate – fortunate in escaping capture – and soon manoeuvred himself into power as First Consul of the Republic. Two years later the army he had left to its fate was defeated by a British force landing at Aboukir Bay among the charred wrack of Nelson's victory.

Meanwhile Nelson – now Baron Nelson of the Nile and Duke of Brontë in Sicily – had succumbed to the extravagant praises which had poured in from every quarter since his victory, and the idolatry he had met at Naples, whence he had come with his squadron after making good the worst battle damages at Aboukir. At Naples he

The ravishing Emma, Lady Hamilton.

Sir William Hamilton,
Emma's husband.

had come again under the spell of the ravishing Emma, Lady
Hamilton – this time as a hero whose name was ringing around the
world – whose fame aroused in Emma's breast such

> fervour caused by agitation and pleasure. God, what a victory! Never,
> never has there been anything half so glorious, so compleat. I fainted
> when I heard the joyfull news, and fell on my side and am hurt … My
> dress from head to foot is alla Nelson. Even my shawl is in blue with gold
> anchors all over. My earrings are Nelson's anchors …

The hero had been enchanted. Basking in her full-blooded warmth
and the glitter and frivolity of the Neapolitan court, so far removed
from his father's vicarage in Norfolk, the rigours of a man of war, and
the correctitude of his wife whose cool nature had never matched
his own exuberance of spirit, tasting absolute fulfilment in glory, he

had become a caricature of self-indulgence and vanity, according to Sir John Moore, 'covered with stars, medals and ribbons, more like a Prince of Opera than the Conqueror of the Nile'. After encouraging the King of Naples in a disastrous attempt to drive the French from Rome – losing Naples itself when the French retaliated – after conducting Mediterranean naval operations with quite uncharacteristic indolence and lack of fire or flair, even acting as if the preservation of the Neapolitan Court, now in Palermo, were more important than the destruction of a French fleet sent into the Mediterranean from Brest, disobeying repeated orders from a new Commander-in-Chief, he became the despair of his friends. Finally, in 1800, he travelled home across Europe with Emma, now his mistress, and the aging Sir William Hamilton. In each capital his visit turned into a 'triumph'; behind the public adulation 'Society' remarked his vainglory and his enslavement to Emma, whose lowly origins, coarseness and capacity for drink and 'guttling' added spice to stories of the absurd figure he was cutting. Although he was received in Yarmouth and London with the most extravagant public acclaim, many of the great were cool. The King snubbed him.

'Admiral Nelson recreating with his brave lads after the Glorious Battle of the Nile' is the caption to this piece of heroic licence; in fact he was recreating with Emma.

Chapter 5

Copenhagen

By the winter of 1800 the second Coalition of Monarchies had collapsed in the face of resurgent French armies, and once again Great Britain found herself fighting alone – this time against the formidable will and enmity of Bonaparte, First Consul and real master of the Republic. In addition, the naval blockade by which Britain sought to prevent France and her allies from obtaining supplies by sea had led to friction with neutrals, notably the countries bordering the Baltic, whose exports of pine for masts and yards, flax for cordage and canvas and numerous other naval stores were vital for all maritime powers. Bonaparte, playing on this disaffection, had persuaded the Tsar of Russia – the most powerful of all the nations concerned – to lend his weight to the creation of a Northern Alliance which would refuse to recognise the rights of belligerent nations to stop and search or seize neutral ships. This alliance, known as the 'Armed Neutrality', consisted of Russia, Prussia, Denmark and Sweden; their fleets in combination could back up the declaration with force.

Britain could not accept such a state of affairs without giving up one of the chief advantages her command of the sea had won. The commercial blockade had almost immobilised the main hostile fleets through lack of masts and spars; if the Baltic traders were to be allowed through freely, France and Spain would be able to re-equip their squadrons in all the major European ports from Holland right around to the Adriatic, and prepare more huge invasion expeditions. In the long run, without her most effective sanctions against Bonaparte, Britain would be powerless against his ambitions. In the early spring of 1801, while the Russian squadrons were still locked in harbour by ice, a strong British force was prepared for the Baltic under the command of Admiral Sir Hyde Parker. British diplomats were already in Copenhagen attempting to break the 'Armed Neutrality' by negotiation with the Danes, who had the most efficient fleet and most commanding position across the entrance to that sea; the fleet was to provide a forceful demonstration of British power and, if the talks failed, to destroy the Danes' capacity to protect their merchantmen. Hyde Parker's secret instructions directed him to await the outcome at Copenhagen, whether 'by amicable arrangements or by actual hostilities'; then proceed to Reval 'to make an immediate and vigorous attack' upon the main Russian fleet, thence to Cronstadt to do the same with the Russian squadron there, 'in general by every means in his power to attack and endeavour to capture or destroy any Ships of War or others belonging to Russia, wherever he can meet with

The elderly and irresolute Admiral Sir Hyde Parker, who eventually gave Nelson his head at Copenhagen.

137

them, and to annoy that Power so far as his means will admit' –
thence back to Sweden to deal with her in the same way. However,
if Denmark or Sweden or both 'relinquished their present hostile
plans against the rights and interests of this country' it was his duty
to afford them 'every protection in his power against the resentment
and attacks of Russia'.

By entrusting to Sir Hyde Parker a task of such huge consequence,
such breath-taking arrogance, such determination to take ultimate
risks – for the Baltic supplies were vital to the Royal Navy – the
Admiralty misjudged sadly. He lacked the ability to analyse and

Hyde Parker's Baltic fleet sails for Copenhagen past the guns of the Castle of Kronenburg.

grasp the essentials of a problem – let alone one of this magnitude. He lacked experience of fleet action, hence the ability to evaluate the risks, and lacking both he lacked the power of decision. For the fighting part of the business, the Admiralty – St Vincent as First Lord now – sent him Lord Nelson as second-in-command.

Nelson, by this time, had broken finally with his wife; his passion for Emma Hamilton, who had just borne him a daughter, Horatia, raged fiercely. Tossing far away from her in the leaking cabin of his 98-gun flagship, *St George*, he was tormented by jealousy; she had become linked in his mind with lecherous ambitions on the part of

139

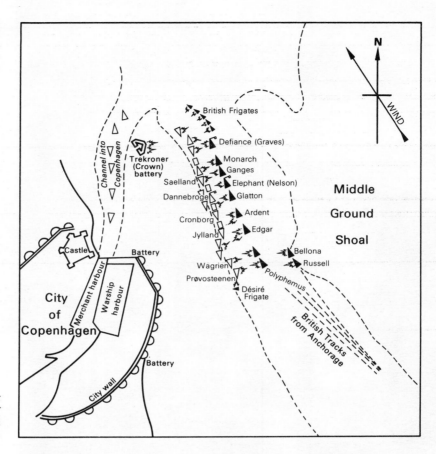

N
WIND

British Frigates

Defiance (Graves)

Trekroner
(Crown)
battery

Monarch
Ganges

Saelland

Elephant (Nelson)

Dannebroge

Glatton

Cronborg

Ardent

Jyllan

Edgar

Middle
Ground
Shoal

Bellona

Wagrien

Russell

Prøvosteenen

Polyphemus

Désiré
Frigate

British Tracks
from Anchorage

Channel into
Copenhagen

Castle

Battery

Merchant harbour

Warship
harbour

City
of
Copenhagen

Battery

City wall

Map 6
Opening of the Battle of
Copenhagen, 2 April
1801.

the Prince of Wales – 'May God blast him! He will propose if you –
no, you will not try; he is Sir William's guest . . . God strike him
blind if he looks at you!' He ate little, wrote her agonised letters
declaiming his carnal passions with uninhibited imagery, his
eternal love in heart and mind. Despite his agitation those friends
who had thought his talents lost to the service since ensnared with
Emma were wrong; he had regained all his old ardour for action
and his sure judgement. The natural eagerness and vivacity of his
character still delighted his captains, officers and ship's company.
And although Hyde Parker looked on him as a dangerously melo-
dramatic egotist whose only thought was personal glory – and
perhaps the humiliation of his Commander-in-Chief – and treated
him with haughty disdain, not showing him his orders or discussing
the great affairs on which they were embarked, Nelson had a far
surer grasp of the objects of the expedition than he. While Parker
delayed in England, not anxious to enter the Baltic until he heard

140

Above After the epic duel between the *Brunswick* and the *Vengeur du Peuple*, the *Vengeur*, her bilges riven, fills and sinks.

The gigantic Spanish prizes captured at the Battle of St Vincent.

Overleaf The *Vrijheid*, totally dismasted, will not surrender to Captain Bligh's *Director* towards the close of the battle.

the result of the negotiations with the Danes, Nelson believed the right thing was to take the fleet straight through the Sound and anchor under the walls of Copenhagen; 'It would be a bold Dane who would put his name to a paper which would in a few moments involve his master's Navy and I hope his capital in flames.' It would also serve to prevent the Danes making additional preparations for the defence of the city.

Nelson hinted to St Vincent that Sir Hyde was dallying, as a result of which the fleet at last sailed, arriving in the Cattegat on 19 March. Still Sir Hyde hesitated to pass through the narrows to Copenhagen. Nelson wrote to Emma, 'to keep us out of sight is to seduce Denmark into a war'. By then it was too late; negotiations had failed, the British Minister had been handed his passport, equivalent in the eyes of the British representative to a declaration of war, and Sir Hyde was instructed to execute his orders. Confronted with the need to act, he called Nelson to conference at last. The British diplomats from Copenhagen were also brought in to describe the political position and the defences the Danes had been mounting for the past weeks. Nelson's keen questions to them on the exact disposition of the battleships and his spirited attitude to attacking won Sir Hyde over – as his clear mind and eagerness had won over all his previous commanders-in-chief. 'I have every reason to believe that Sir Hyde has found it not necessary to be high to me,' he wrote afterwards. 'His conduct is certainly the very reverse of what it was.' The following day he wrote to him, 'the more I have reflected, the more I am confirmed in opinion, that not a moment should be lost in attacking the enemy: they will every day and hour be stronger: we shall never be so good a match for them as at this moment.' He tried to prod Sir Hyde into action by impressing the importance of their mission: 'Never did our Country depend so much on the success of any Fleet as on this,' and after outlining his plans for attacking from the weaker, southern end of the floating gun batteries which had been described by the diplomats, he outlined a scheme, if the wind were westerly, to sail up the Baltic instead and attack the Russian fleet at Reval. For Russia was 'the enemy most vulnerable and of the greatest consequence for us to humble'. Sent by St Vincent as a fighting admiral, he showed strategic and political insights of which his chief was incapable. 'The measures might be thought bold, but I am of opinion the boldest measures are the safest; and our country demands a most vigorous exertion of her force, directed with judgement.'

Eventually Sir Hyde Parker, who had been inclined to wait in the Cattegat until the opposing fleets should come out to him, was

The British – and German – view of Bonaparte after he had made himself Emperor –' ... by the wrath of Heaven Emperor of the Jacobins, Protector of the Confederation of Rogues, Mediator of the Hellish League, Grand Cross of the Legion of Horror ... Arch Chancellor of Waste-Paper Treaties, Arch Treasurer of the Plunder of the World ...'

145

persuaded to sail up the sound, past the gun batteries commanding both shores to Copenhagen. The passage was made on 30 March through the middle of the two-and-a-half-mile narrows in perfect safety despite an 'uninterrupted blaze' of guns from the Danish shore. When the fleet had come to anchor some eight miles northeast of Copenhagen, Hyde Parker, Nelson, the other subordinate admiral, Graves, the commanding officer of the military force with the fleet, and several captains went aboard a frigate to inspect the defences from close to. Hyde Parker found the line of battleships, frigates, hulks, floating batteries and gunboats all supported by a great fixed battery, Trekroner – called by the British the Crown – 'more formidable than we had reason to expect'. So did Graves. Nelson wrote to Emma that it looked formidable to 'children at war', but 'to my judgement with ten sail of the line I think I can annihilate them'. The truth lay somewhere between these estimates. The Danes had their ships and floating defences in two divisions, one east of the Crown battery in a compact line extending southwards covering the walls of the city, the other west of the battery, moored alongside the channel leading in to the port. Both these divisions were under separate naval commanders under the overall direction of the Crown Prince of Denmark who was organising the defence of the city. However, the Crown Prince had made no arrangements to co-ordinate the divisions, nor to use either as a mobile defence to support whichever part of the system was attacked. Had either of these steps been taken the volume of fire power afloat, supporting and supported by the great Crown

battery, which mounted seventy cannon, would have been as formidable as Sir Hyde Parker feared.

Once again he resorted to a council of war aboard the *London*. Once again Nelson, impatient to attack without delay, made light of all difficulties. The military commander noted:

> During this Council of War the energy of Lord Nelson's character was remarked; certain difficulties had been stated by some of the members relative to each of the three Powers we should either have to engage in succession or united in those seas. The number of Russians was in particular represented as formidable. Lord Nelson kept pacing the cabin, mortified at everything which savoured either of alarm or irresolution. When the above remark was applied to the Swedes, he sharply observed, 'The more numerous the better', and when to the Russians, he repeatedly said, 'So much the better, I wish they were twice as many, the easier the victory, depend upon it'.

In the end Parker's captain of the fleet, who had served in several fleet actions under Keppel, Rodney and Howe, joined Nelson in support of an immediate attack, and Parker agreed to let Nelson have twelve of the line, together with all frigates and smaller craft, to make the attempt, as he had proposed, from the weaker, southern end of the line. Parker himself was to support him from the northern end with a squadron which included the three-deckers; they would have difficulty in the shoal water Nelson would have to negotiate in his attack from the south. In a very handsome manner, quite the reverse of his earlier attitude, he left all details of the main, southern assault to Nelson.

The Danish floating defences before Copenhagen.

To reach a position for his attack Nelson had to sail down a channel separated from the inner channel in which the Danish defence line was moored by a large 'middle ground' shoal, the position of which was not known with any certainty; again there were no reliable charts in the fleet and the Danes, naturally, had removed all buoys and marks. That night he had the pilots and masters with lead lines, notebooks, compasses with shaded candles and casks to serve as buoys, put out in boats with muffled oars to sound and mark the middle ground. More soundings were taken the next day and marking vessels anchored to guide the fleet, and in the afternoon of 1 April, to the accompaniment of rousing cheers from all ships, Nelson's division weighed and sailed down the marked channel to anchor safely off the southern end of the middle ground as darkness fell.

Now that action was imminent Nelson was in the highest spirits and invited Graves and several of his most intimate friends among the captains to dine with him aboard the 74-gun *Elephant*, to which he had transferred his flag several days earlier because of her shallower draft; her captain was Thomas Foley, who had led into Aboukir Bay three years before. When the party broke up about nine o'clock and the captains 'each with feelings of admiration for their great leader and with anxious impatience to follow him into the approaching battle', returned to their ships, Nelson set to work to prepare detailed plans. He sent Hardy – whom he had rescued from the Spaniards before St Vincent – to sound the channel towards the Danish line as close as he could go without detection, and with Foley and one other frigate captain, Riou, whom he had come to admire greatly, he started to thrash out the order of battle and the precise opponent for each ship in it. Hardy returned before midnight and reported sufficient water right up to the southern-most enemy, but the detailed orders were not finalised until one a.m., when clerks were called into the after cabin to make a copy for each captain. As they worked on by lantern-light until dawn, he called out to them every half hour or so to 'Hasten. For the wind is coming fair!' It came around to south-south-east, the ideal quarter for the approach.

By seven a.m. lieutenants from each ship had been summoned to the *Elephant* and furnished with a copy of the orders; at eight o'clock the signal was made to prepare for battle and for anchoring with the springs (hawsers) on the anchors and the cables led out through stern ports. As the drums beat their urgent call to action stations and the men responded eagerly, Nelson conferred with several of the more experienced masters and pilots. He found them

148

annoyingly hesitant to lead in close to the enemy line; contradicting Hardy's findings they believed that the lightened Danish ships and the shallow floating batteries had been moored in shoal water which would not be deep enough for the heavier British line ships. Eventually he found a man, Brierley of the *Bellona*, prepared to lead, whereupon the others agreed to follow, and at 9.45 the signal was hoisted to weigh anchor, leewardmost ships first. The *Edgar* had been chosen to head the line, and she was soon under way standing before the wind to round a lugger which had been anchored to mark the south-western end of the middle ground.

As she approached the southernmost enemy hulk, the former first-rate *Prøvesteenen*, now cut down to two decks with one stump mast, she came under fire from a shore battery south of the line, then from the 40- (English) pounder and 26-pounder guns on the *Prøvosteenen*, and the fire spread gradually up the line. The *Edgar* closed in perfect silence except for brief orders to the quarter-masters, loud commands to the parties working the yard, and as at Aboukir the continuous chanting of the leadsmen in the larboard chains. 'She made a beautiful and solemn spectacle' against the white smoke puffs, the castellated battlements, the forest of masts and spars in the commercial port, close green roofs, towers and spires and wind-mills of the queen of northern cities, alive now with anxious spectators crowding every vantage point. Above, the sky was heavy with cloud. As she wore to the northwards, bringing her own guns in bearing, she replied to the *Prøvesteenen*'s fire, and passing on to her appointed position opposite the fifth in the line, engaged in succession the *Wagrien*, a two-decked hulk, and two single-decked fully-rigged transports before cutting away her anchor and bringing up abreast and some two hundred yards off her own opponent, the two-decked *Jylland*. By this time the *Ardent*, some distance astern, was also exchanging broadsides with the rear ships as she made up towards her place just ahead of the *Edgar*. Others were manoeuvring in her wake.

Splendidly as the leaders closed and anchored in position, else-where things were already going wrong. The *Agamemnon*, supposed to be fifth in the line and to place herself opposite the *Prøvesteenen*, was unable to weather the end of the middle ground. She had been the northernmost ship in the crowded anchorage during the night, and despite sending kedge and stream anchors away in boats and trying to warp herself down channel to windward, she could not get far enough south to round the shoal. Nelson signalled the *Poly-phemus* to take her place. As this ship steered through the press waiting to follow the prescribed order, and neared the dense smoke 149

At the height of the
battle; the view from
the rear of the line.
To the right the
Bellona and *Russell*
aground, at the left the
frigate *Désirée* taking up
a position to rake the
Prøvesteenen.

which had spread over the whole of the Danish rear, the *Bellona*,
attempting to make her way up to the centre of the Danish line well
outside the engaged British ships, ran up hard on a spur of the
middle ground. Nelson, who had already warned her by signal that
she was standing in to danger, ordered her to engage the enemy
closer, and shortly afterwards made the signal general to all ships.
The *Bellona* replied that she had struck on a shoal. Meanwhile the
150 flagship passed between her and the other engaged British ships.

Nelson, considerably agitated as he saw his already outnumbered force reduced by two, ordered his ship placed in the *Bellona*'s berth opposite a single-deck transport and a floating battery mounting twenty-four 26-pounders, and tried to get his Master to lead in closer. But the pilot insisted that the water shoaled towards the enemy line and eventually dropped anchor in just over four-and-a-half fathoms still more than 250 yards from their opponents. The stump of Nelson's right arm worked restlessly. The *Ganges* came up 151 astern and he hailed her from the gangway, directing her to take the 74-gun *Saelland*, his own ship's planned opponent; as others came up he directed them all to one position astern of the place they had been ordered to take up. So the fire spread towards the head of the Danish line and the immensely powerful Crown battery.

For some reason, perhaps because he had under-estimated the strength of the defences, or because his twelve ships were out-numbered by the hulks and floating batteries, Nelson had made no attempt to concentrate his force and overwhelm sections of the enemy in detail. Thus the battle resolved itself into a number of grim, static and in places very equal duels. The Danes, although lacking the training and experience of the British crews, were defending their city from brutal aggression and fought with great spirit; their floating batteries whose bulwarks rose scarcely six feet above the water were difficult to hit, while they had far larger, higher targets in the British 74's. And because of their superiority in numbers they were in places able to concentrate two or three batteries on one British ship.

Added to this, another British 74, the *Russell*, in the dense smoke of the battle, had followed the *Bellona* on to the middle ground shoal – leaving Nelson with only nine out of his original twelve of the line in their planned positions. For some while, as the destruction and casualties mounted terribly on both sides, as the British hove their dead through the ports, carried the wounded below, filled the gaps in the guns' crews from the upper-deck men or Marines, while the Danes replenished their powder and shot and replaced their casualties by boats from the shore, the issue seemed to hang in the balance, Nelson, pacing the starboard side of the *Elephant*'s quarterdeck as a shower of splinters was struck from the mainmast, observed with a smile to the officer commanding the military, 'It is warm work. And this day may be the last to any of us at a moment.' The officer later recalled that as Nelson stopped to turn at the gangway 'he used an expression never to be erased from my memory, and said with emotion, "But, mark you, I would not be elsewhere for thousands!"'

The British frigates, meanwhile, joined in to fill up the gaps left by the ships aground. The 44-gun *Désirée* anchored across the southern end of the Danish line where she could rake both the *Prøvesteenen* and the next along, *Wagrien*; as both these were also under fire from the battleships anchored abreast of them and from the grounded *Bellona* and *Russell*, they received an unintended concentration and suffered severely, frequently catching alight. The other five British frigates stood up to the head of the line where a Danish frigate and a two-decked hulk had no opposition – because of the re-arrangement consequent on the groundings. They anchored in a line abreast of these two unmarked vessels, and, despite being exposed to the great Crown battery half a mile away, began to reduce them.

Ever since the attack had begun Hyde Parker and his division had been attempting to beat down to support Nelson's division from the north, but with wind and current against them had made little progress. By noon, with the smoke and thunder of battle still heavy, no chance of his own ships coming into action before the evening and no sign of the Danish defences giving way – indeed the massed guns of the Crown battery were erupting in rapid time – Hyde Parker had become very worried about the result. The three British battleships aground and out of the main action did nothing to reassure him; he held anxious conference with his senior officers about ordering a retreat, both to save Nelson's ships from being beaten so close to the shore and inevitably falling into enemy hands, and to save Nelson himself from the whole responsibility of failure. Before doing so he allowed his flag captain to put off in a small boat for the *Elephant* to find out from Nelson himself exactly how things were going. The boat made slow progress, and by 1.30, with the battle still shrouded in thick smoke and no news from Nelson, Hyde Parker could wait no longer; he ordered signal 39, 'Discontinue the engagement' made general to all ships, and emphasised it with two guns.

But by this time the Danish floating defences were crumbling. The superior training of the British guns' crews had overcome the stubborn spirit of the defenders at most points; the two rear hulks, exposed to an overwhelming British concentration, were still firing a few slow pieces, but their casualties were enormous and many of their guns and carriages wrecked. The two transports to the north of them had been beaten out of the line, as had one similar transport in the centre; the Danish flagship, *Dannebroge*, was burning uncontrollably after receiving incendiary shells from her opponents' carronades – which were now loaded with grape and depressed to scour the men from a floating battery on her quarter. Near by in the centre the frigate *Cronborg* had been so heavily hit that all but a handful of her men and one surviving officer had abandoned her, while at the rear of the line the five British frigates had forced their two opponents to submit. The Danes were still ferrying fresh men and powder out to those batteries and hulks continuing the struggle, two of the British battleships near the head of the line were fiercely engaged and suffering heavily and the Crown and other batteries

153

The heroic defence of Floating Battery No. 1 at Copenhagen.

ashore were keeping up a heavy bombardment, nevertheless the backbone of the defence had been broken. Nelson, with his intuitive sense of the balance of battle, knew it had tipped decisively in his favour. When the *London*'s signal 39 was reported to him as he paced the quarterdeck he appeared to take no notice. At the next turn the signal lieutenant asked him whether he should repeat it.

'No – acknowledge it,' he replied, then called out after him, 'Is number 16 [for closer action] still flying?'

The lieutenant replied that it was.

'Mind you keep it so,' Nelson said, continuing his pacing considerably agitated, the stump of his arm working again. 'Leave off the action!' he shrugged. 'Now, damn me if I do!' And turning to Foley, he said, 'You know, Foley, I have only one eye – I have a right to be blind sometimes.'

'And then with an archness peculiar to his character, putting the glass to his blind eye, he exclaimed, "I really do not see the signal!"'

Ahead of the *Elephant* Rear-Admiral Graves repeated signal 39, but also left number 16 flying in a superior position at the main topmast head – an act of considerable moral courage – and continued the action, as did all the other battleships. But at the extreme northern end of the line the frigates obeyed the Commander-in-Chief and hauled off, accompanied by a destructive fire from the Crown battery; Captain Riou, who had impressed Nelson so much during the preliminary operations, was killed during this withdrawal.

The cannonading continued in places for some time, but within half an hour it was apparent that the Danish floating defences were broken. The flaming *Dannebroge* drifted out of control, menacing those still moored, her men leaping from gunports and chains, and many of the British ships sent boats to rescue survivors. However, British boarding parties approaching those hulks which had ceased fire were repulsed by small arms and by guns from the shore, and at length, after repeated further broadsides had failed to subdue these last acts of defiance, Nelson, sickened by the slaughter of already beaten enemies, and angered by such a violation of the code of warfare, called for writing materials and retiring into his stern gallery penned a brief note to the Danish Crown Prince: 'To the brothers of Englishmen, the Danes …' He had directions to spare Denmark when no longer resisting, he stated, but if firing were continued, he would burn all the prizes taken 'without having the power of saving the brave Danes who have defended them'. To give the message consequence and to impress his opponent that it was not composed in haste, he folded it carefully and had a man sent to fetch wax and a candle so that he could seal it with his arms. The man was killed on the way. When this was reported to him he ordered another sent; at length the wax was brought to where he stood with the purser by the casing of the rudder head and he took great pains to ensure that his arms were stamped with a sharp impression. The letter was taken by boat under a large white flag of truce to one of the unengaged battleships still anchored to the west of the Crown battery in the main channel leading into the port of Copenhagen, and from thence to the Crown Prince ashore. The Prince sent one of his aides to find out exactly what Nelson proposed, afterwards agreeing to negotiations with Hyde Parker. As his aides set out by boat for the *London*, now anchored with her division some three miles north-east of the Crown Battery, the guns 155

At the height of the Battle of Copenhagen; the view from the city.

at last fell silent, the thick banks of smoke began to drift and thin northwards, and a pale sun, which had broken through earlier, lit the scarred and broken hulks, the cold green waves afloat with wreckage, bodies, a myriad boats ferrying wounded defenders ashore or British taking armed parties to possess the prizes. In the centre of the scene the *Dannebroge*, her hull scarcely visible under smoke, rolling, glowing with flame from every port and aperture, finally blew apart. After the roar of the explosion and the gunfire that had shaken the air continually since the morning, the quiet was intense. Along the waterfront men with strained, white faces were carried ashore; women pressed, searching for their own and weep-

ing; rumours spread; news and pure speculation became confused.

After protracted negotiations aboard the *London* and at the palace in Copenhagen, where Nelson went to conduct the talks on Hyde Parker's behalf, the Danes – under threat of an immediate bombardment of the city now that the southern defence line had been destroyed – signed an armistice, whereby they agreed to suspend their alliance with Russia and make no fleet movements or preparations for fourteen weeks, also to supply the British fleet. With this agreement behind him, Nelson was anxious to get up the Baltic to Reval to deal with the Russians, the root of the Northern Alliance. But as before Hyde Parker delayed interminably – this time fearing the Swedish fleet at his back. It was not until the Admiralty had received first-hand reports of the indecision preceding the Copenhagen operations, as a result of which they relieved Hyde Parker of his command and appointed Nelson to succeed him, that the fleet was able to proceed. This was on 5 May; by then it had been learned that Tsar Paul had been assassinated. His successor was already negotiating to end the 'Armed Neutrality', and Nelson arrived at Reval only to be informed in a curt note that his presence was not compatible with friendly relations between Russia and England. He immediately weighed and sailed back down the Baltic; on the 19th the 'Armed Neutrality' was dissolved.

It was not long before Nelson, fretful at the inactivity which came with accord, was allowed to return to Emma and Horatia.

How large a part 'Copenhagen' played in the ending of the 'Armed Neutrality' is not clear. It was a powerful demonstration of British resolve. Yet the real target should have been the Russian fleet – as Nelson had suggested from the first. And as it turned out the Tsar Paul had been murdered even before the battle took place. Yet the action gave another boost to British naval prestige – and to Nelson's, adding embroidery to the legend that already surrounded his name. Tactically the battle held no lessons; it had been a drawn-out struggle of attrition with victory going to the more concentrated fire-power of the British line ships over their generally weaker opponents. The cost had been heavy for the numbers involved; for the Danes 476 killed, 559 wounded at the lowest estimates, and for the British almost as many, 256 killed, 688 wounded. The worst sufferer on either side was the *Monarch* (220 killed and wounded), which had been exposed to the fire of the Crown battery as well as a floating battery and a blockship; the *Edgar* which had led the way had also suffered severely with 142 casualties. Rear-Admiral Graves, who had voted against the attempt originally, but served Nelson bravely after the decision had gone against him, wrote to his brother of the carnage: 'I am told the Nile was nothing to this.' Of the attempt itself, which he still thought 'a losing game in attacking stone walls' – and of course none of the shore batteries, the Castle or the Crown battery had been affected in the battle – 'Considering the disadvantages of navigation, the approach to the enemy, their vast number of guns and mortars on both land and sea, I do not think there ever was a bolder attack. It was worthy of our gallant and enterprising little hero of the Nile. Nothing can exceed his spirit.'

158

London Pub.^d by G. Humphrey 27 St James's St April 3.^d 1821.

Dido in Despair.

Ah! where, and ah where, does my gallant Courier lie,
For me does he oft on his downy pillow sigh,
I left him on the Continent, to claim my half-a-Crown.
And I wish to my heart, I could have him here alone.

Nelson was allowed only three weeks' leave before St Vincent directed him to take charge of a special squadron of frigates and small craft for defence of the east coast and Channel against invasion. For Bonaparte, having forced the latest continental combination against him to accept peace terms with a series of brilliant campaigns which left him master of continental Western Europe, had turned his attention to the major enemy – now the only one. The flotillas of small craft which he had put in hand before his Egyptian adventure were augmented by scores of flat-bottomed craft urgently constructed in the Dutch, Belgian and northern French ports, large rowing pinnaces, fishing smacks, luggers and gun brigs, and massed chiefly in Boulogne and the ports of Flanders, protected by coastal batteries. His idea was to slip them across the Straits of Dover one long, dark night near the close of the year and land some thirty thousand troops on the Kent coast for a rapid march on London. This was his declared aim. Whether he really thought the plan feasible without at least temporary battle-fleet command of the Channel is doubtful. It is more probable – at least after the collapse of the 'Armed Neutrality' and the return of the British fleet to home waters – that his very public preparations were designed to impress the British government with a sense of urgent danger so that he might persuade them to make peace on better terms for France than otherwise seemed likely. He needed peace. The naval blockade had bitten deeply. His ports were starved of naval stores, his merchants of colonial produce, the French flag had been swept off the seas, French industry consequently cut off from supplies and markets by the absolute British command of the oceans – all this at a time when British oceanic trade and industry were expanding and flourishing as never before. Bonaparte needed peace similarly to draw strength from the world, to replenish, to make use of his vastly expanded continental coastline, to rebuild his naval power so that eventually he could destroy the ring of tough oak which cramped his soaring ambitions for mastery.

Although the British government and southern England generally thought his threat to London alarmingly real, Nelson, after reconnoitring the embarkation ports with his frigates and making an abortive and costly attempt to destroy the massed small craft in Boulogne, thought the invasion impossible without battle-fleet support. The strong tides and poor sailing qualities of most of the small craft made the plan dependent on extraordinarily favourable winds and weather, and he suspected that St Vincent held him suspended off the east coast simply to keep him away from Emma.

St Vincent insisted that his presence there was essential to 'tranquillise the public mind'.

He was released by the success of Bonaparte's peace campaign. A preliminary agreement whereby practically all the colonial possessions of France, Spain and Holland seized during the wars, were returned to their former owners, was signed in October 1801, and ratified in March the following year. Bonaparte had his breathing space; Great Britain, weary of the endless war, had opportunity to continue expanding her world trade and smoking factories without the cost of convoys and loss to the privateers which still escaped the naval net; Nelson had the prospect of domestic bliss with Emma.

Earlier he had bought Merton Place – whose seventy acres of grounds extended across what is now Merton High Street – for just such a purpose. Now he installed Emma, furnished the rooms in extraordinarily poor taste – 'not only the rooms but the whole house, staircase and all, are covered with nothing but pictures of her and him, of all sizes and sorts, and representations of his naval actions' – and preening himself in public acclaim and her crude flattery, enslaved by her warmth and fire, entertaining extravagantly, he lived to the dismay of many of his real friends, but to his own great content, with the woman and the little girl who meant more to him even than fame.

Chapter 6

Trafalgar

THE TIMES

For 7th NOVEMBER. 1805

BATTLE OF TRAFALGAR

CAPTURE OF FRENCH AND SPANISH FLEETS

DEATH OF NELSON

List of Killed and Wounded

Nelson was called away in the spring of 1803. Bonaparte had revealed his designs to shut Britain out of continental markets and at the same time build up his naval strength to win a great colonial empire, and in May the British government declared war. The Admiralty, still under St Vincent, was prepared; immediately, blockading squadrons stationed themselves off the principal French ports. Nelson was selected for the Mediterranean command, and by July was lying with nine of the line off Toulon; he seized a base off Sardinia to refit and provision his force and over the next twenty months in the sudden, gusting weather of the Gulf of Lions, maintained an 'open' blockade, trying – without success – to entice the French fleet out for a decisive battle. He saw out one French Commander-in-Chief, Latouche-Tréville, who died in the summer of 1804, as Nelson thought, 'of walking so often up the hill to the signal post to watch us'. Vice-Admiral Villeneuve, who had escaped from the Nile, was appointed to succeed him; he was an able but not an inspiring officer, one who saw his difficulties, especially the inexperience of his men and the renown of his opponent, larger than his opportunities.

Nelson continued his teasing open blockade, never setting foot on shore himself, but organising fresh food and changes of scene and activity for his men which kept the sick list remarkably low. By now scurvy, the great scourge of blockading ships, had been much reduced in the British fleets. Regulations of 1799 for the supply of fresh lemon juice to all ships had been proved effective by St Vincent himself when in command of the Channel Fleet before becoming First Lord. Other improvements in hygiene and the supply of fresh food, partly as a result of the mutinies, partly as a result of more humane attitudes of the age, had raised health standards. In any case Nelson was in the tradition of Howe and St Vincent in caring for his men. As he wrote at the time:

> The great thing in all military service is health. You will agree with me that it is easier for an officer to keep men healthy than for a physician to cure them. Situated as this fleet has been without a friendly port where we could get all things necessary for us, yet I have, by changing the cruizing ground, not allowed the sameness of prospect to satiate the mind – sometimes by looking at Toulon, Villefranche, Barcelona and Rosas; then running around Minorca, Majorca, Sardinia and Corsica; and two or three times anchoring for a few days and sending a ship to the last place for onions, which I find the best thing that can be given to seamen; having always good mutton for the sick, cattle when we can get them, and plenty of fresh water . . .

A poster advertising *The Times* to commemorate Trafalgar. In fact, *The Times* of that date was not able to report the number of casualties due to bad weather conditions.

163

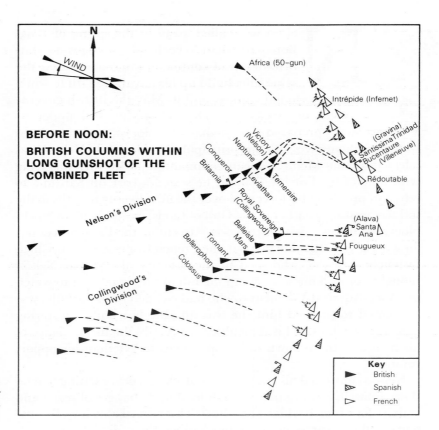

N

WIND

BEFORE NOON:
BRITISH COLUMNS WITHIN
LONG GUNSHOT OF THE
COMBINED FLEET

Africa (50-gun)

Intrépide (Infernet)

(Gravina)
Santissima Trinidad
Bucentaure (Villeneuve)

Rédoutable

Conqueror
Britannia
Neptune
Victory (Nelson)
Leviathan
Temeraire

Royal Sovereign (Collingwood)

Nelson's Division

Belleisle
Tonnant
Mars

(Alava)
Santa Ana

Bellerophon

Fougueux

Colossus

Collingwood's Division

Key
British
Spanish
French

Map 7
Opening of the Battle of
Trafalgar, 21 October
1805.

It was on one of these excursions off the Spanish coast at the end
of March 1805 that Villeneuve slipped out of Toulon with eleven of
the line and, shaking off shadowing frigates during the night, succeeded in evading Nelson, and escaping from the Mediterranean
to Cadiz. Spain had declared war against Britain in December, and
Villeneuve's orders were to pick up what Spanish ships he could
from Cadiz, then sail across the Atlantic to the West Indies. This
was part of a complex plan devised by Bonaparte – whom the
French now called the Emperor Napoleon, although the British
never recognised him as such – to draw British blockading squadrons away from Europe and at the same time to concentrate his own
separated fleets into one huge armada which would descend on the
English Channel to cover an invasion of England. This time he was
in deadly earnest. His flotilla of over two thousand specially designed
small craft waiting at Boulogne and other Channel ports could lift
over 150,000 men, together with siege ordnance and sappers' tools,
stores and nine thousand horses. Some ninety thousand troops were
164   waiting nearby; the remainder were quartered within easy march.

All that was necessary was for a sufficient concentration of battle-ships to obtain command of the Channel for the four days – at the least – which would be required to get all the boats across to the East Kent coast.

To obtain this, Bonaparte had ordered his main Brest fleet under Admiral Ganteaume to break out – without getting engaged in a fight with the blockading force – cross Biscay to release battleships blockaded in Ferrol, and take them with him across the Atlantic to Martinique. There, if all went well, he was to meet another squadron which had already broken out from Rochefort, and also Villeneuve with whatever Spanish ships he had managed to collect from Cadiz. While British squadrons chased to the West Indies to find them all, the huge combined fleet under the supreme com-mand of Ganteaume was to sail east, drive off or destroy whatever British forces were concentrated in the western approaches and enter the Channel.

Almost the only part of this scheme that went right was Ville-neuve's break-out. While Nelson cruised in the central Mediter-

Napoleon gazes across the Channel from Boulogne.

165

ranean, believing he might be bound for Naples or Egypt again, Villeneuve picked up one other French and six Spanish ships of the line under Admiral Don Federigo Gravina and disappeared into the Atlantic. Nelson eventually learnt of his passage through the Straits, and hearing reliable reports that he was bound for the West Indies, chased there, arriving three weeks after him in early June. By this time Villeneuve had received fresh orders consequent on Ganteaume's failure to break out from Brest; he was to sail back to Ferrol and chase off the small blockading squadron there, join the Spanish ships inside to his flag, then go north, chase the blockaders from Brest, release Ganteaume and so enter the Channel. And he had no sooner learnt of Nelson's arrival in the West Indies than he started back across the Atlantic. Nelson followed him, now only four days behind. But as Villeneuve headed for Biscay, and Nelson turned back for Cadiz and Gibraltar, he failed to make contact. However, Villeneuve's more northerly track was reported to the Admiralty by the brig Nelson had sent home with despatches and as a result the First Lord made a masterly redeployment of forces which brought fifteen of the line into Villeneuve's track a hundred miles off Cape Finisterre. After a confused engagement in fickle airs and thick mist two Spanish ships struck and Villeneuve retired with the rest of the Combined Fleet into Vigo.

The indecisive engagement confirmed Villeneuve in his worst fears about the ships he commanded; since the first gales of the voyage he had complained of inexperience and clumsiness in his

Blockade of Brest; the storm-bound ships that stood between Bonaparte and dominion of the world.

crews, which contained very few real sailors, and of the bad materials supplied by the dockyard; now he could add the poor quality of his officers, shortage of all provisions and the abysmal health of his men. It is a measure of the vast gap that separated the French and British services that while Nelson, after his twenty months' blockade followed by a chase twice across the Atlantic – 'an effort', one admirer wrote, 'such as never was realised in former times, nor I doubt will ever again be repeated by any other Admiral' – arrived back at Gibraltar with his crews in spanking health and spirits, Villeneuve had no less than 1700 on his sick lists; eight hundred of them had to be put ashore.

From Vigo, in compliance with his orders, Villeneuve sailed to Ferrol, whose blockade had been lifted to provide the fifteen ships which had engaged him earlier; there he found yet another set of orders, this time unusually elastic: if he could not release Ganteaume from Brest, he was to sail for the Channel ports northabout around the west of Ireland and Scotland, pick up a squadron of the line waiting at the Texel, then descend on the Channel from the east. However, if 'through incalculable events' this became impossible, he was to sail for Cadiz where in due course 'a mass of imposing forces' would be assembled. Villeneuve, lacking any confidence in his spars, officers or crews, burdened with sickness, lacking provisions, knowing that Nelson was back at Gibraltar and that all surprise had been lost, only had to see some frigates on the horizon and learn from a Danish captain the planted false intelligence that they were the advance guard of a British fleet of twenty-five of the line, to choose the easy course – back to Cadiz. There he was found and blockaded.

Nelson, meanwhile, weary and extravagantly dispirited by his failure to bring the Combined Fleet to action, suffering the sleeplessness, loss of appetite and stomach cramps that always afflicted him at such times, returned home to tumultuous receptions at Portsmouth and along the London Road to 'dear, dear Merton', Emma and Horatia.

On 1 September the frigate *Euryalus* arrived in the Solent and her captain, Blackwood, immediately set out for London with the news of Villeneuve's arrival in Cadiz. On the way at five in the morning he stopped at Merton. Nelson, already up and dressed, guessed that he came to tell him of the Combined Fleet – 'I think I shall yet have to beat them,' he said. Soon afterwards he followed Blackwood to

the Admiralty where the First Lord, now Lord Barham, re-appointed him to the Mediterranean command.

Twelve days later, in the evening, he said a prayer by Horatia's bed as she slept, then entered a coach for Portsmouth and drove away from

> all which I hold dear in this world, to go to serve my King and Country. May the Great God, whom I adore, enable me to fulfil the expectations of my Country; and if it is His good pleasure that I should return, my thanks will never cease being offered up to the Throne of His Mercy. If it is His good Providence to cut short my days upon earth, I bow with the greatest submission, relying that He will protect those so dear to me.

His flagship, *Victory*, had been prepared for sea and she sailed the morning after his arrival, 14 September, joining the blockading force off Cadiz on the 28th. 'The reception I met with on joining the Fleet caused the sweetest sensation in my life. The officers who came on board to welcome my return forgot my rank in the enthusiasm with which they greeted me.' His brief rest at Merton had refreshed him, and the sight of a forest of masts within Cadiz heightened his ardour to bring Villeneuve to action. Plans for the meeting had been maturing since his blockade of Toulon – before that while chasing Brueys to Alexandria, before that even while pouring over *An Essay on Naval Tactics*, written by an enthusiastic amateur tactician, John Clerk of Eldin in Scotland, or studying the brilliant results of Camperdown, which bore out Clerk's thesis in striking fashion. He intended to divide his force into two groups – with a smaller group to windward to reinforce one or other if he had sufficient ships – and throw both upon the enemy to cut through and overwhelm smaller sections of their line before the unattacked third or so – the van in his latest ideas – could come round to their support. This would bring on mêlées in which the two thirds of the enemy attacked would be unable to escape very close action – in which case the superior British close-range gunnery would inevitably prevail. To ensure that the enemy had little time to counter or retire while his own ships had the maximum time to complete the business – 'for half a victory would but half content me' – he intended to dispense with the usual preliminaries of forming and dressing line or lines, and simply make the order of sailing the order of battle. 'No one day can be long enough to arrange a couple of fleets and fight a decisive battle according to the old system,' he had explained to one of his most trusted captains, Keats, in the grounds at Merton earlier that month. 'I shall go at them at once if I can – about one third of their line from their leading ship. What

Opposite The picture of his daughter, Horatia, which Nelson carried with him.

169

do you think of it?' And before Keats had time to reply, 'But I'll tell you what I think of it. I think it will surprise and confound the enemy. They won't know what I am about. It will bring forward a pell-mell battle, and that is what I want.'

When he came to explain these ideas to the captains of the fleet assembled before Cadiz, inviting half of them to dine the night after he joined – his forty-seventh birthday – the other half on the following night, they were fired with his enthusiasm. He described the scene to Emma. 'It was like an electric shock. Some shed tears and all approved. It was new – it was singular – it was simple.'

Later he wrote the ideas out in some detail in the form of a memorandum, a copy of which was given to each captain; it was made clear that captains were to look to their own group as their rallying point, but if in doubt 'no Captain can do very wrong if he places his ship alongside that of an enemy'. One group, 'the lee line', would be 'under the entire management' of his second-in-command, in fact his very old friend, Cuthbert Collingwood. In his intended attack from windward Nelson would bring the fleet in its three groups nearly within gunshot of the enemy's centre, then give a signal for the lee line to put their helms up together, setting all sail, even studding sails 'in order to get as quickly as possible to the Enemy's line, and cut through beginning with the twelve ships of the Enemy's rear'. As the lee line was to consist of sixteen ships this would bring a twenty-five per cent superiority upon the enemy rear. 'The remainder of the Enemy's Fleet, 34 Sail, are to be left to the management of the Commander-in-Chief, who will endeavour to take care the movements of the Second-in-Command are as little interrupted as is possible.' To ensure this, Nelson probably intended a feint towards the van: he certainly intended that his attack, when it came, would fall on the enemy centre 'so as to ensure getting at their Commander-in-Chief, on whom every effort must be made to capture'.

These then were the principles: to lose no time in manoeuvre, to overwhelm the rear and centre by involving them in close mêlées from which they could not escape, to trust each British ship to assist her consorts, and those least damaged in the first encounters to repulse any counter-attack from the enemy van. To these principles he and his captains adhered in the battle which took place off Cape Trafalgar later that month – but to no other principles of tactics or of battle by land or sea before or since.

Meanwhile Bonaparte, confronted with yet another coalition against him organised by the British, and despairing of his admirals' ability to give him command of the Channel, had abandoned his

Opposite Admiral Cuthbert Collingwood, who came to Nelson's aid at St Vincent, who led the lee line at Trafalgar, and whose record of continuous, devoted service in the subsequent close blockade of the enemy is unsurpassed. One of the outstanding officers of an outstanding era.

invasion plans and marched towards the new enemy, Austria, sending orders for Villeneuve's Combined Fleets to enter the Mediterranean and land their troops on the flank of his advance near Naples. At the same time he made it clear that the time for French fleets to evade their enemy in pursuit of the mission with which they were entrusted was over; Villeneuve was ordered not to hesitate to attack superior or equal forces and to engage in fights *à outrance*. The Emperor would not count the loss of ships so long as they were lost with glory! Subsequently Bonaparte received reports from his military commander aboard the flagship, *Bucentaure*, alleging that the failure of the Combined Fleet's mission had stemmed from Villeneuve's cowardice – whereupon he sent another flag officer to replace him.

Villeneuve had been preparing for sea to carry out his new orders long before he heard rumours of his impending replacement, but no doubt these hardened his resolve, and when on 19 October the wind came into the north-east, fair for leaving Cadiz, he gave the order to sail. The circumstances were peculiarly favourable: he knew Nelson had detached six of the line to Gibraltar for fresh provisions so that his own thirty-three of the line would face only twenty-seven British. But he had no illusions; he knew that, short of a miracle, his miscellaneous ships' companies, completed with raw scourings from the streets of Cadiz, would be no match for the long-experienced, superbly drilled men waiting just over the horizon under the command of the most aggressive and consistently victorious admirals of his – or any other – day. He knew too that Nelson had discarded all formal tactics and would not form line of battle; instead he would 'seek to break our line, envelop our rear, and overpower with groups of his ships as many of ours as he can isolate and cut off'. Villeneuve lacked all confidence in his own captains' ability to come to the rescue of such isolated groups; he sailed in pursuance of his orders, hoping that in defeat his service would at least acquire honour.

Captain Blackwood in the frigate *Euryalus*, tacking close in to Cadiz at daylight, saw the French and Spanish t'gallant yards across, and soon the headmost under sail standing for the harbour mouth. He sent his companion frigate towards Nelson to repeat his signals, sent small craft to Gibraltar and nearby squadrons with the news, and prepared to shadow. Keeping close by Villeneuve all that day and the next, sending reports to Nelson who manoeuvred in the offing, anxious not to frighten Villeneuve back to port, he brought the two fleets together during the night of 20 October. When dawn broke over a misty sea on the morning of the 21st, Nelson could see

the masts and sails of the Combined Fleet some twelve miles away over the eastern horizon, evidently forming line of battle, heading southwards. He made a general signal to form the order of sailing in two columns, then to wear and sail large on an east-north-easterly course – towards the rear of the enemy. The wind was very light and variable from north of west; there was a long, deep swell – token of a severe storm centre in the Atlantic moving in upon them. The ships spread all sail to catch the breeze and moved heavily in slow time, lifting and leaning over the great combers which drove towards the

Captain Blackwood of the frigate *Euryalus*; Nelson trusted him so much that he permitted him to use his (Nelson's) name to order ships to the support of others if necessary at Trafalgar.

173

Sketch by Turner showing the quarterdeck of the *Victory*, looking aft to the stern windows as it would have looked when cleared for action – but without guns, boarding nets, fire buckets etc.

enemy, and gradually they formed two irregular, dispersed lines ahead, the larboard one headed by the *Victory*, the starboard by Collingwood's three-decker, *Royal Sovereign*, both winged with studding sails.

Drums beat to quarters, port lids were hauled up, the guns, already loaded with two roundshot, were run out, their carriages thudding against the port sills; loading gear was laid ready, tackles flaked, flints checked, firing lanyards fastened, match casks placed and filled with brine, boarding pikes and cutlasses stacked amidships, decks sanded, fearnought screens hung around the hatches and damped. Men peered out of the ports at the line of distant masts rising from the haze on the starboard bow. It would be many hours yet; some started sharpening cutlasses, others 'polishing the guns as though an inspection was about to take place instead of a mortal combat', others dancing a hornpipe to a fiddler's tune.

Presently ships' bands were mustered and rousing, martial tunes struck over the water, heightening impatience for battle. The sun climbed over the haze; its light glistened on the rippled, deeply heaving blue sea.

Nelson was in high spirits – although fretful at the slow progress they were making. He had called his frigate captains aboard the *Victory*, and as he searched the distant masts for clues to Villeneuve's strength and intentions he quizzed them on the number of prizes they expected, insisting that nothing less than twenty would satisfy him. He had told Hardy, the *Victory*'s captain, the same figure earlier. He wondered aloud what Villeneuve would make of his novel approach in two columns.

As they watched the enemy ships, doubled or trebled in many places with long gaps between groups, it became apparent that they were wearing; after a long while they had come right round on

Thomas Masterman Hardy, Nelson's Flag Captain at Trafalgar.

175

the other tack with their heads to the north, the leading ships close on the wind, the centre and the straggling rear – which had been an advanced squadron to windward of the rest – making sail to close the gaps so that the formation resembled a crescent with the concavity towards the British. They were evidently making back for Cadiz. Yet the wind was too light, and it was veering into the north-west heading them off. In fact Villeneuve, divining Nelson's intention to concentrate on his rear, had gone about simply to prevent it.

Collingwood had made a signal for his division to form the starboard line of bearing – a bow and quarter line to starboard of the *Royal Sovereign* so that his ships would be in line ahead when they hauled to the wind on reaching or passing through the enemy line – but it soon became evident that the *Royal Sovereign* had no intention of shortening sail to allow the ships astern to catch up sufficiently to form a proper line of bearing – 'no one day can be long enough' – and as they watched she was actually drawing away from her next astern, the *Tonnant*. Nelson, after making a general signal to alter the course of the fleet one point to larboard to cut off Villeneuve on his new heading, signalled Collingwood to put other ships between him and the *Tonnant* if the latter could not keep up. Collingwood complied: the *Belleisle* crept up into second place and then the *Mars* came up astern of her. Still the *Royal Sovereign* continued to draw away; as a midshipman remembered it:

> There is now before me the beautiful, sunshiny morning of the 21st October; the sea like a mill pond, but with an ominous ground swell rolling in from the Atlantic. The noble fleet with royals and studding sails on both sides, bands playing, officers in full dress, and the ships covered with ensigns in various places . . . I see before me at the end of half a century dear old Cuddie (as we called Collingwood), walking the break of the poop with his little triangular, gold-laced cocked hat, silk stockings and buckles . . .

Nelson kneels in prayer by his stern windows before Trafalgar: 'May the Great God whom I worship, grant to my Country, and for the benfit of Europe in general, a great and glorious Victory …'

Nelson, the slight breast of his blue and gold-trimmed frock coat ablaze with all his stars and orders, his cocked hat worn unfashionably athwartships with a green eyeshade protruding to shield his good eye, went below to his cabin, now clear of furniture and open to the whole sweep of the deck, and kneeling at the stern, wrote in his diary:

> May the Great God whom I worship, grant to my Country, and for the benefit of Europe in general, a great and glorious Victory, and may no misconduct in anyone tarnish it; and may humanity after Victory be the predominant feature in the British Fleet. For myself, individually, I commit my life to Him who made me, and may His blessing light upon

my endeavours for serving my Country faithfully. To Him I resign myself and the just cause which is entrusted to me to defend. Amen. Amen. Amen.

He had Hardy and Blackwood witness his signature to a codicil to his will, leaving Emma Hamilton 'a legacy to my King and Country, that they will give her an ample provision to maintain her rank in life', also his daughter Horatia. Then, accompanied by Hardy, lieutenants and aides, he made the rounds of the decks, reinforcing the men's eagerness and optimism with his own inimitable enthusiasm. 'My noble lads, depend upon it, this will be a glorious day for England, whoever lives to see it. I shall not be satisfied with the twelve ships taken at the Nile!'

Aboard other ships captains talked to their men in their different styles: 'I have only to recommend silence and strict attention to the orders of your officers. Be careful to take good aim, for it is to no purpose to throw your shot away . . .' Collingwood, elevated by the brilliant scene as the French and Spanish ships stood boldly to take the attack and manoeuvred to close their gaps and thin the bunches, addressed the officers gathered about him after his tour of inspection. 'Now gentlemen, let us do something today which the world may talk of hereafter.' Similar inspiration livened the enemy preparations; in the *Redoubtable*, one of the best-trained of all the French ships, the fervently aggressive captain, Lucas, strutted the decks preceded by drums and fifes and a standard bearer with the Imperial Eagle, and found everywhere burning enthusiasm. Lucas believed in boarding and in Cadiz had drilled his sharpshooters and boarding parties with thorough regard for every detail; now they reminded him to lay the *Redoubtable* aboard the enemy and they would carry her decks. A similar enthusiasm prevailed in the flagship, *Bucentaure*. The Imperial Eagle was paraded before Villeneuve, greeted by repeated roars of 'Vive L'Empereur!' and 'each one of us putting our hands between the Admiral's, renewed our oath to fight to the last gasp'.

So the long hours of the approach drew out. The poorer sailers in the British columns were now a long way astern of the bunched leaders, wallowing deeply as the wind dropped to near calm in places, fickle light breaths just sweeping the water with catspaws, the sun bright through crowded canvas. Nelson, noting the ominous westerly trend of the high clouds, told his signal lieutenant, Pasco, to make a preparative signal for the fleet to anchor at the close of day. He also signalled Collingwood that he intended to push through the enemy's line to prevent them from getting into Cadiz.

As Collingwood was heading for the sixteenth ship from the rear, the magnificent black-painted flagship of the Spanish Vice-Admiral Alava, the two columns diverged until the *Royal Sovereign* was a mile to starboard of the *Victory*. Nelson and the group of frigate captains, the surgeon, chaplain and other officers and aides searched for Villeneuve's flagship in the bunched centre. The magnificent *Santissima Trinidad*, flagship of the Spanish Admiral Gravina, was plain to see, her hull bright with four broad bands of crimson interspersed with ribbons of white, colossal figures representing the Holy Trinity under her bowsprit. But they could not find Villeneuve. At length, as the *Royal Sovereign* slid within long gunshot of the enemy rear, Nelson decided to inspire the fleet with his own confidence. 'Suppose we telegraph "Nelson confides that every man will do his duty"?' One of the party about him suggested 'England' instead; he agreed, and going up to the poop called to Pasco, 'I wish to say to the fleet, "England confides that every man will do his

'England expects ...'

The two columns of British ships break through the line of the Combined Fleet at Trafalgar; in fact the British columns were far more dispersed than the artist suggests.

duty.'' He added, 'You must be quick, for I have one more to make, which is for close action.' Pasco replied that it would be quicker to substitute 'expects', which was in the numerical code, for 'confides' which would have to be spelled out.

'That will do, Pasco. Make it directly.'

The signal men hastened to prepare the hoists.

ENGLAND EXPECTS THAT EVERY MAN WILL DO HIS DUTY.

Shortly afterwards, as the enemy fleet ran up their colours simultaneously to rolls of drums, crashes of muskets and first one, then others opened fire on the *Royal Sovereign*, Nelson took leave of the frigate captains. Last to go was Blackwood. Nelson gave him permission to use his (Nelson's) name to signal any of the rear ships

as they came into action to do what he thought best – extraordinary confidence and latitude. It was evident by now that the fight would be fierce; the enemy was not flinching; the lines of broadsides towards which the *Victory* was gliding had clouded with the first puffs of smoke, shot was raising splashes in the sea ahead; soon Blackwood would be able to see far more of the general situation than anyone aboard the flagship. As the captain went over the side to return to his frigate Nelson had a sudden premonition of his own death. 'God bless you, Blackwood,' he said. 'I shall never speak to you again.'

A mile to the south, the *Royal Sovereign*, her studding sails drawing and way ahead of the rest of her division, her guns' crews flat on deck as the volume of enemy shot increased, firing only an occasional gun to provide smoke cover, closed the *Santa Ana* and the *Fougueux* astern. 'What would Nelson give to be here!' Collingwood exclaimed to his captain. As his starboard guns came in bearing of the four ships astern of the *Santa Ana*, he gave permission to return the enemy fire. Nelson was watching with admiration. 'See how that noble fellow Collingwood takes his ship into action! How I envy him!'

The *Royal Sovereign* broke the line close under the *Santa Ana*'s stern at about noon; the guns of her larboard broadside began to crash out; the rich carvings, heavy black timbers, delicate panes of the Spanish stern galleries, the great timber cross hanging over her taffrail, were shaken, torn to dust and splinters; the balls thudded on between the decks, smashing through the heavy beams, beam knees, against guns, overturning carriages, swathing paths of mangled flesh and shattered fittings right up to the bows. Shortly afterwards the *Royal Sovereign*'s warm starboard guns poured into the *Fougueux* whose own crews had been firing for some fifteen minutes already. The ship shook and heeled under the storm of ball and grape. The flagship rounded up close under the *Santa Ana*'s lee quarter, men aloft cut the studding sails away and they fell into the water or over the hammock netting. Collingwood called to a lieutenant to help him rescue one that fell near by. Smoke rose in thick clouds about them as the larboard guns' crews slipped into their deadly drill. A French 74 to leeward began to engage from the bow, and the *Fougueux*, coming up on the lee quarter, was also firing into them; the masts and rigging, badly cut during the slow approach, were shot to pieces and the scarlet Marines drawn up on the poop suffered heavily. More Spanish ships and a Frenchman became visible ahead also firing at them and the *Santa Ana*, crippled as she had been by that first raking broadside, kept up a stubborn resistance with a few guns. For an age it seemed as if they were fighting alone and completely surrounded; then the *Belleisle* broke through the smoke astern and relieved them, and shortly afterwards the *Mars*; in succession the other leading ships of the division which had spread to starboard came to close action through the whole of the enemy rear which broke up into clouding clusters of vessels.

To the north of them, Nelson had made out Villeneuve's flagship, *Bucentaure*, just astern of the *Santissima*, and had altered slightly to starboard from his original course for the enemy van, intending to break the line under her stern. The earlier fire from nearly all the leading enemy had been ineffectual, but as the *Victory* neared the cluster of ships in the centre about the two great flagships she came under a close concentration which tore the sails and rigging, shattered the wheel and took a heavy toll of men, including Nelson's private secretary, cut almost in half by a ball as he talked to Hardy on the quarterdeck. 'This is too warm work, Hardy, to last for long,' Nelson said as he paced beside him. As the ship surged and swelled towards the *Bucentaure*'s stern, Captain Lucas of the *Redoubtable*, following in Villeneuve's wake, pressed on sail and closed until his jibboom was almost scraping the flagship's taffrail. It was impossible to get through between the two; Nelson gave Hardy leave to run either aboard, 'It does not signify which.' Hardy chose the smaller *Redoubtable*, ordered the helm to starboard. Slowly the bluff bows came round and the foremost larboard guns opened into Villeneuve's quarter from less than a hundred yards, then as the ship passed across the French stern and drove into the *Redoubtable's* bows the rest of the larboard broadside poured round-shot and grape through the stern timbers and windows, raking from end to end and from so close that the British yardarms caught the French gaff vangs as they passed; dust from the pulverised wood-work blew back over the officers on the *Victory*'s quarterdeck. At the same time the *Victory*'s mizen topmast fell; her main t'gallant, fore

The *Victory* rakes Villeneuve's flagship, *Bucentaure*, with her larboard broadside as she drives into the *Redoubtable's* bows, forcing her way through the line. The *Téméraire* can be seen following her at the left of the picture.

topmast and all her upper yards and rigging were cut and hanging in confusion.

The *Redoubtable* shuddered and swung to starboard under the impact of the *Victory*'s bows, the yards and rigging of the two ships locked, and Lucas' well-trained men flung grapnels; held side by side, the *Victory* overlapping astern, the two ships fell off the wind together. Lucas had ordered his lower gun ports closed to prevent the *Victory*'s men boarding through them; now he had the trumpet sound for the boarders, and they swarmed up from below, along the gangways, up on the boats and booms and netting above, into the rigging up to the poop; his picked sharpshooters were already firing down from the tops at the British quarterdeck and forecastle guns' crews, the pacing officers and the Marines drawn up along the

hammock nettings and returning the musketry fire; others of Lucas'
men lobbed grenades which were exploding throughout the flagship's upper decks in flame and smoke. Casualties mounted, clog-
ging the ladders down to the cockpit; the dead were tossed into the
sea. Through it all the surviving British carronade crews on the
quarterdeck and forecastle which towered above the *Redoubtable*'s
decks, loaded their warm pieces with grape and canister, heaved
them smartly outboard, and scarcely bothering to point, swathed
paths of death and agony through the parties of boarders climbing a
few yards from them. Below, the guns' crews of the heavy pieces,
now unopposed, sponged and loaded with flexible rope-handled
implements and wrecked the French gun decks with repeated
broadsides, not a shot of which could miss.

The *Britannia* and
Conqueror follow the
Victory towards the
mêlée about the enemy
flagships.

Meanwhile the three-deckers which had been following closely in the *Victory*'s wake had surged through the gap left astern of the *Bucentaure*; first the *Téméraire*, then the *Neptune* raked the French flagship, the latter ranging up her lee side, the former carrying on to attack a group of French and Spanish two-deckers to leeward. After them came two 74's which followed the *Neptune* up the lee side of the *Bucentaure* to engage the *Santissima Trinidad* and her two Spanish 'seconds', and then the three-decker *Britannia* pushed into the embattled scene around the two chief enemy flagships. Meanwhile a British 64-gun ship which had been absent from the fleet that morning joined in from the north, while various shattered enemy vessels from the rear, still making sail on the larboard tack, drifted up from the mêlée about the *Royal Sovereign*. Villeneuve's formation was broken beyond recall; only in the van, still standing northwards, was there any semblance of order. To windward five of Nelson's division of battleships and four of Collingwood's wallowed towards the battle with all sail set; the furthest was still two miles off.

It was at this time, about 1.15, that one of the sharpshooters from the *Redoubtable*'s mizen top, swaying not more than fifteen yards above the *Victory*'s quarterdeck, fired a ball which struck Nelson's left epaulette and, carrying pieces of gold lace and silk with it, ploughed down through his shoulder and lung, and striking off the second and third ribs, fractured the sixth and seventh vertebrae

Villeneuve's line is broken into a series of confused mêlées; in the foreground, the fore-castle party of the *Victory*.

before coming to rest in the muscles below his shoulder blade. He fell to his knees, then collapsed on his left side. 'They have done for me at last,' he breathed as Hardy, who had been pacing beside him, turned and bent. 'My backbone is shot through.' He was carried below to the cockpit, a handkerchief covering his face so that the guns' crews would not be discouraged. 'Ah, Mr Beatty,' he said to the surgeon as he was laid in one of the midshipman's berths, undressed and covered with a sheet, 'You can do nothing for me. I have but a short time to live; my back is shot through.' After he had described his symptoms, gushes of blood every minute within his breast, no feeling in the lower part of his body, his breathing difficult and accompanied by intense pain about that part of the spine he was sure the ball had struck, the surgeon realised his case was hopeless.

'I am gone,' Nelson repeated. 'I felt it break my back,' and in quick agitated sentences, broken by pain, 'Remember me to Lady Hamilton! Remember me to Horatia! Remember me to all my friends!' The ship's chaplain, who had hurried from the cockpit overwhelmed by the scenes of horror immediately before Nelson was hit, but had returned with Nelson, now ministered to him as the surgeon left to attend the scores more of clamouring wounded. Above them the deck shook to repeated discharge of cannon, thud of trucks on the planking.

Looking forward from the quarterdeck of the *Victory* as Nelsons falls to one of the *Redoubtable's* trained marksmen.

These were the larboard guns firing into the enemy ships supporting the *Bucentaure*; the starboard guns were silent for the *Redoubtable* had ceased resistance. The *Téméraire* had fallen across the French ship's bows on her disengaged side soon after Nelson fell, and added her fire to the *Victory*'s, afterwards swinging alongside to starboard so that the three ships drifted together, the smaller *Redoubtable* between the British three-deckers, their fallen masts and yards all interlocked. When the *Téméraire* shortly hailed Lucas to submit and halt the carnage, he could do nothing else.

> Our ship was so riddled that she seemed to be no more than a mass of wreckage. All the stern was absolutely stove in, the rudder stock, the tiller, the stern post, the helm-port and wing transoms, the transom knees were in general shot to pieces; the decks were all torn open; all the guns were shattered or dismounted by the shots or from the two ships running us aboard; the two sides of the ship, all the lids and bars of the ports were utterly cut to pieces; four out of our six pumps were shattered as well as our ladders in general, in such a way that communication between the lower and upper decks was extremely difficult; all our decks were covered with dead, buried beneath the debris and the splinters from different parts of the ship. Out of the ship's company of 643 men we had 522 disabled, 300 being killed and 222 wounded, amongst whom were almost all the officers.

The *Bucentaure* and *Santissima Trinidad*, raked and engaged alongside by a succession of British ships, were in almost as bad a plight. The Spanish flagship's masts had all gone by the board; cut close to and below the deck and with the rigging hanging useless, she had rolled them overboard: 'Her immense topsails had every reef out, her royals were sheeted home but lowered and the falling of the mass of spars and rigging, plunging into the water at the muzzles of our guns was one of the most magnificent sights I ever

beheld,' wrote a British officer in the *Conqueror*. The French flagship had only her foremast standing when she surged into the stern of the *Santissima* and the shock sent that, too, crashing down. Helpless and surrounded by British ships, with fresh ones still coming into the action, both flagships eventually struck; other wrecked and dismasted ships in the rear had already hauled down their colours, as had the *Fougueux*, which had fallen aboard the disengaged side of the *Téméraire*, making a pontoon of four more or less wrecked ships; soon the *Santa Ana* too hauled down her colours after a long and hopeless resistance to the *Royal Sovereign*.

The scenes which greeted the British boarding parties were horrific. Aboard the *Bucentaure*, where Villeneuve lamented his fate as one of the very few unscathed officers, 'the dead, thrown back as they fell, lay along the middle of the decks in heaps and the shot passing through had frightfully mangled their bodies. An extraordinary proportion had lost their heads.' Between decks in the

The 74-gun *Redoubtable* (Captain Lucas) sandwiched between the British first-rates, *Victory* and *Téméraire*, puts up a heroic resistance.

189

great *Santissima* the beams 'were covered with blood, brains and pieces of flesh, and the after parts of the decks with wounded, some without legs, some without an arm'. Overall were 'fragments of spars, splinters of wood, thick hempen cables cut up as corn is cut by the sickle, fallen blocks, shreds of canvas, bits of iron'. Water poured in through scores of holes and crevices as she wallowed in the trough of the swell; the decks above the swirling water were tacky with blood which had made strange patterns through the sand. The first task of the boarding party was to throw the remains of 254 dead over the side.

Meanwhile the ships of Villeneuve's van had put about at last. Four formed line and passed down some distance to windward of the mêlée around the flagships, firing into the thick of it until confronted with the last two of Nelson's division – so far unengaged – still making towards the battle; after a brief cannonade on opposite tacks the four sailed on and, judging the battle already lost, retired. Another four bore off to leeward straight away to join a group retiring from the centre and rear, and only one, the *Intrépide*, steered straight to the support of the Commander-in-Chief. It was far too late. She was surrounded by the less-damaged British and overwhelmed 'after one of the most gallant defences I ever witnessed'. Her captain, Infernet, and his ten-year-old midshipman son were treated with the greatest respect when they were taken aboard the *Orion*.

The *Intrépide* was the last ship to strike, some time after five o'clock. Nelson was not alive to hear the cheers which greeted it.

The close of the battle; British frigates close to tow off prizes – in the foreground the wrecked *Fougeux* with the terrible total of 532 killed and wounded; the scenes which greeted the British boarding parties were horrific.

But he had died in the knowledge of a brilliant victory. Hardy, visiting him a short while before as the firing slackened, had been certain of fourteen or fifteen prizes.

'That is well,' Nelson had replied, his voice catching with pain. 'But I had bargained for twenty.' Then with a touch of the old fire, '*Anchor*, Hardy, anchor!' He could feel the swell rising beneath the *Victory*'s timbers.

Hardy had replied that he expected Collingwood to take over the direction. 'Not while I live, I hope, Hardy,' and trying in-effectually to raise himself on one arm. 'No – do *you* anchor, Hardy. For if I live I'll anchor.' Shortly afterwards, feeling he had little time left he had told Hardy to kiss him. The captain had knelt and kissed his cheek, then after staying a while in silence by his beloved chief, had returned to the deck. Nelson called out after him, 'Hardy, if I live I'll bring the fleet to anchor,' and continued after he had passed up the ladder, 'If I live I'll anchor.' Afterwards his pain had increased, and thirst. Between calling for the chaplain to rub his chest, give him drink and fan him, speaking in rapid, broken syllables, he repeated his bequest of Lady Hamilton and Horatia as a legacy to the country, and said over and over, 'Thank God – I have done my duty.'

Blackwood, who had been towing the now dismasted *Royal Sovereign* up towards the mêlée about the flagships until the cable was parted by shot from the van ships passing to windward, hastened aboard the *Victory* as Nelson died.

> I do not hesitate to say that in life I never was so shocked or completely upset as upon my flying to the *Victory* . . . to find Lord Nelson was then at the gasp of death . . . so entirely am I depressed with the private loss I have had, that really the Victory and all the prize money I hope to get appear quite lost by the chasm made by Lord Nelson's death . . . I can scarcely credit he is no more . . .

Hardy was in similar distress, so too Collingwood when Black-wood told him the news: 'I cannot tell you how deeply I was affected,' he wrote later to his father-in-law, 'my friendship for him was unlike anything I have left in the Navy.' And to the others he repeated, 'There is nothing left like him.'

Now Commander-in-Chief, Collingwood shifted his flag from the unmanageable *Royal Sovereign* to Blackwood's frigate, and set about securing the prizes and having the dismasted and crippled British ships taken in tow. In all there were eighteen enemy hulks rolling deep in the mounting swell amongst the wreckage of their masts and spars; one, burning to the water and surrounded by boats rescuing survivors from the sea, shortly blew up. Of the rest of

Villeneuve's thirty-three of the line, four from the van were making off southwards and eleven were struggling north for Cadiz in the light breeze. Few of the British ships were in a fit state to chase, and with the rocks of Trafalgar a bare eight miles to leeward and all signs pointing to an imminent storm, Collingwood gathered the fleet and the prizes under tow in the dusk and made the signal for preparing to anchor. Only a few ships were able to do so; many had had their cables shot through or their anchors carried away, and throughout the night most remained under sail, beating off the land, their exhausted crews manning the pumps continuously, splicing the rigging, stopping shot holes, repairing sails, rigging jury masts.

The following day the wind rose with heavy rain, and by noon they were tossing in the grip of violent squalls from the south-west. It was the beginning of a week of almost continuous gales during which only a fortunate shift of wind prevented the damaged British ships and all the prizes from being driven ashore; seamanship and resolve were tested to the limit. Damaged masts fell, tows had to be cast off, anchors cut away, upper-deck carronades thrown into the sea to decrease topweight, while aboard two of the prizes the prisoners rose against their captors and re-took the ships; one got safely into Cadiz, the other drove on the rocks together with other prizes which had to be abandoned. Collingwood was forced to order most of the rest to be destroyed and eventually only four of the seventeen got into Gibraltar after desperate exertions. None of the British ships were lost – a feat of seamanship equalling the brilliance of the original victory, and one which filled French and Spanish with enthusiastic admiration.

The loss was high; the British suffered 1,214 killed and wounded, the Combined Fleet some 2,330; several of those ships like the

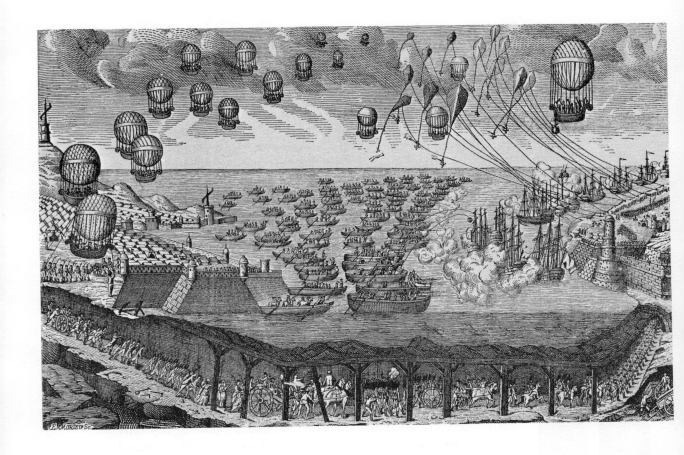

Redoubtable which had defended themselves most heroically having
an appalling rate of casualties, far greater even than the two
principal enemy flagships: the 74-gun *Fougueux*, for instance, had
the terrible total of 532 killed and wounded. The worst sufferers in
the British fleet, mainly the leaders of the two divisions, were not
nearly so hard hit; the *Royal Sovereign* had 141 casualties, the *Victory*
and the *Téméraire* some 120 each; worst hit was the *Colossus*, fifth in
Collingwood's division, with 160 killed or wounded.

The result was not quite the annihilation Nelson had desired, but
it was the end of Villeneuve's fleet. As Collingwood wrote to the
British Minister at Naples, 'The Combined Fleet is annihilated. I
believe there are not more than four or five ships in Cadiz which can
be made ready for sea. I understand there are neither masts, sails
nor cordage to refit them – a shattered fleet and empty magazines.'

Nelson's sword.

Trafalgar was not the end of the naval war. Bonaparte never gave up his ambition to destroy and invade Great Britain. Right up to the end he continued building ships of the line and hatching new coalitions of powers against the island nation. It was still necessary for British fleets to blockade his naval arsenals, and Collingwood wore out his life in the task, still necessary to convoy merchantmen against French privateers, which increased their depredations after the failure of their battle fleets, necessary for frigate captains to keep the seas swept of enemy shipping, for the Admiralty to stage another 'Copenhagen' – although not such a desperate affair as Nelson's – to remove another Danish fleet from a hostile coalition; the coasts of England still had to be protected, for which purpose chains of Martello towers around the southern and eastern coasts were added to the naval defences; vigilance could not be relaxed until Bonaparte himself was defeated ten years later. But it was the command won during Nelson's time which allowed Great Britain to continue the struggle against all his machinations, allowed Wellington's armies virtually uninterrupted supplies during the Peninsular campaign which bled France before Waterloo, and allowed British merchant shipping, trade and industry to expand at a faster pace than ever it had during peace, while France stagnated. And by the end of the wars Great Britain had laid the industrial and overseas bases for the most powerful world empire in history – 'The Empire of the Seas'.

Although Trafalgar did not end Bonaparte's power, and only increased his determination in the long run to rebuild his fleet and conquer Great Britain, it did mark the end of the period of great fleet actions, setting the seal in dramatic style on a period of triumph which has few if any parallels outside the legends of ancient Rome. And the legend of invincibility won during those years persisted for well over a century, giving the Royal Navy a remarkable moral position; in Nelson himself its captains had an example of matchless inspiration. As Collingwood, his very old friend, wrote:

He possessed the zeal of an enthusiast, directed by talents which nature had very bountifully bestowed upon him, and everything seemed as if by enchantment to prosper under his direction: but it was the effect of system and nice combination, not of chance. We must endeavour to follow his example, but it is the lot of very few to attain to his perfection.

Select Bibliography

Actions

E. Desbrière (transl. Eastwick), *The Naval Campaign of 1805; Trafalgar*, Oxford at the Clarendon Press, 1933.

Col Drinkwater-Bethune, *A Narrative of the Battle ... of St Vincent*, London 1840 & Blackmore, 1969.

C. Ekins, *Naval Battles*, London, 1824.

C. Gill, *The Naval Mutinies of 1797*, Manchester U.P., 1913.

C. Lloyd, *St Vincent and Camperdown*, Batsford, 1963.

C. Lloyd, *The Nile Campaign*, David & Charles, 1973.

D. Pope, *The Great Gamble; Nelson at Copenhagen*, Weidenfeld, 1972.

T. Sturges Jackson (ed.), *Logs of the Great Sea Fights* (2 vols), Navy Records Society, 1899.

O. Warner, *The Battle of the Nile*, Batsford, 1960.

O. Warner, *The Glorious First of June*, Batsford, 1961.

O. Warner, *Trafalgar*, Batsford, 1959.

Post-Trafalgar

R. Glover, *Britain at Bay, 1803–14*, Allen & Unwin, 1973.

Admirals

Sir J. Barrow, *Richard Earl Howe*, Murray, 1838.

G. Bennett, *Nelson the Commander*, Batsford, 1972 (wherein may be found the vast Nelson bibliography).

Camperdown, Earl of, *Admiral Duncan*, Longmans Green, 1898.

G. Newnham-Collingwood, *Correspondence of Vice Admiral Lord Collingwood*, London, 1828.

N. H. Nicolas, *The Despatches & Letters of Lord Nelson*, Murray, 1845.

H. Tours, *Life & Letters of Emma Hamilton*, Gollancz, 1963.

J. Tucker, *Memoirs of Admiral Earl St Vincent*, London, 1844.

O. Warner, *The Life & Letters of Admiral Lord Collingwood*, O.U.P., 1968.

Tactics, Strategy

J. S. Corbett, *Fighting Instructions 1530–1816*, Navy Records Society, 1904.

J. S. Corbett, *Signals and Instructions 1776–1794*, Navy Records Society, 1908.

J. Cresswell, *British Admirals of the 18th Century*, Allen & Unwin, 1972. (Marvellously analytical account disposing of much naval historical dogma; required reading for a proper understanding of tactics.)

A. T. Mahan, *The Influence of Sea Power on the French Revolution & Empire*, 1892.

Gunnery

P. Padfield, *Guns at Sea*, Hugh Evelyn, 1973.

Seamanship

Darcy Lever, *The Young Sea Officer's Sheet Anchor*, London, 1819.

General

E. H. Jenkins, *A History of the French Navy*, MacDonald & Janes, 1973.

P. Kemp, *The British Sailor; a Social History of the Lower Deck*, Dent, 1970.

M. Lewis, *A Social History of the Navy 1793–1815*, Allen & Unwin, 1960.

C. Lloyd, *The British Seaman*, Collins, 1968.

C. Lloyd (ed.), *The Health of Seamen*, Navy Records Society, 1966.

Captain Marryat, *Peter Simple* and other novels.

J. Masefield, *Sea Life in Nelson's Time*, Methuen, 1905.

W. Richardson (ed. Childers), *A Mariner of England, 1780–1819*, Murray, 1908.

W. Robinson, *Nautical Economy, or Forecastle Recollections*, London, 1836.

Select Glossary of Nautical Terms

Bearing: The horizontal angle between an object and a fixed reference point, usually the fore-and-aft line of the ship, or compass north.

Belay: To make a rope fast – usually around a stout wooden (belaying) pin.

Bilge and bilge: An expression to indicate two ships side by side and touching.

Block: Made-up wooden shell (elm or ash) having one or more rollers (sheaves) of lignum vitae or metal fitted internally; used to form purchases to give a mechanical advantage – i.e. block and tackle.

Bowlines: Ropes to the edges of sails to pull the leading edge forward so that the canvas attacks the wind at the proper angle.

Bowsprit: Mast projecting forward from the stem (or bows).

Braces: Ropes to the *yardarms* used to pull the yards around so that the sails attack the wind at the proper angle.

Cartridge: The canvas or paper or flannel bag containing the gunpowder charge for the guns.

Cathead: Timber extending outboard from the side of the forecastle, having sheaves for a purchase used to heave the bower anchors up clear of the ship's side to the position in which they are secured.

Chains: See *Shrouds.*

Close-hauled: Sailing with the yards braced forward to the maximum extent so as to steer as close as possible into the wind (i.e. towards the direction from which the wind is coming).

Double-shotted: Guns loaded with two round shot – the norm for close action – or one round shot, one grape etc.

Dressing the line: Forming a straight line of ships with the correct interval between each.

Fearnought screens: Material screens rigged in action to prevent fire or 'flash' passing down to the ammunition-handling parties or magazines.

Frigate: By this date a single-gun deck vessel, not considered fit to lie in the line of battle; its duties, reconnaissance, towing off ships damaged in battle, convoying merchantmen, engaging enemy frigates and merchantmen, etc. etc.

Gaff vangs: Ropes leading from the peak of the *gaff* (the spar on the mizen mast to which the fore-and-aft sail – spanker or driver – is attached) which guy it to the correct angle to the wind.

Gangways: The narrow decking providing communication along either side of a ship between her forecastle and her quarterdeck.

Halyards: Ropes to hoist sails.

Handspike: Length of timber used as a lever to raise the breech of a gun or to shift the gun carriage when aiming.

Haul to the wind: To point a ship closer into the wind. The closest a ship could sail was about six points ($67\frac{1}{2}°$).

Hawser: Cable-laid rope smaller than the anchor cables, used for mooring etc.

Head gratings: Gratings forward of the bow beneath the bowsprit providing a working platform – also used as 'convenience' for crew (i.e. 'the heads' in nautical parlance still refers to the lavatory).

Helm: Wooden bar fixed through the rudder head (also called tiller) used for angling the rudder; helm 'up' meant moving it towards the windward (therefore high) side of the ship, so turning the bows away from the wind – and vice versa for helm 'down'.

Hulling shot: Shot striking an opponent's hull.

Jibboom: Spar extending forward from the bowsprit.

Kedge anchor: The smallest anchor, often taken out from the ship in boats and dropped so that the ship may heave herself off a shoal or when the wind dies etc; this is known as kedging.

Lanyards: Here the small line attached to a sailor's knife.

Larboard: That side of the ship to the *left* when looking forward.

Lee or leeward: The opposite side to that from which the wind is coming.

Leeway: The ship's drift to leeward of her course.

Line of bearing: Diagonal formation of ships sailing off the wind (i.e. not sailing close-hauled) so that when they haul to the wind they will form a line ahead (i.e. each will be sailing in the wake of her next ahead).

Luff: The leading edge of a sail; hence verb 'to luff up' is to point the ship closer to the wind (see *Close-hauled*).

Masts: The three masts were named from forward, *fore-*, *main-* and *mizen*-mast; above the lower masts were *topmasts*, thus *fore top-mast*, *main topmast*, etc; above these *t'gallant* masts.

Orlop deck: The lowest deck in the ship – above the hold, below the lowest gun deck (and below the waterline).

Poop: The short, uppermost deck at the stern.

Quarter: That part of a ship between the main chains (chains for the main-mast) and the stern; thus a direction some 4 points (45°) abaft the beam (behind a line extending outboard at right angles to the keel at mid-length).

Quarters (Stand to): The position each man takes up for action – with his position go specific duties.

Rake: To fire up the length of another vessel from a position off her bow or stern.

Sails: The lower, and largest sails took their names from the mast, thus *foresail*, *mainsail*, or were known as '*courses*'. Above them were the *fore topsail*, *main topsail* etc.; these had three rows of *reef points*, with which the canvas could be shortened as the wind rose. Above were the *t'gallant* sails, and above them small sails known as Royals. The sails were spread on yards; the yards on the fore and main masts had extensions which could be rigged out for extra canvas, *studding sails*, when the wind was light.

Besides these *square sails* were fore-and-aft sails between the masts, known as *staysails*, also *jibs* right forward.

Scuppers: Channel around outboard edge of deck.

Ship of the line: A ship having at least two complete gun decks, considered fit to lie in the line of battle, a 'battle-ship'. These were rated according to the number of guns carried, the most numerous type being the 'Third Rate' of 74 guns. A 'First Rate' had three complete gun decks and 100 or more guns.

Shiver (Verb): When a sail points too close into the wind and flaps.

Sheave: See *Block*.

Shrouds: Ropes leading from the top of each mast; the lower shrouds lead to chains (links of iron bolted to the ship's side) either side of the hull. The shrouds take the chief strains on their mast, supporting it both sides and from astern (as they lead aft).

Spars: Lengths of timber for masts or yards.

Spritsail: Square sail set below the *bowsprit*.

Starboard: That side of the ship to the *right* when looking forward.

Stream anchor: Usually a rather smaller anchor than the bower anchors, used to steady the ship at a temporary mooring etc.

Tack (Noun): The direction a sailing vessel is moving with reference to the wind; thus on the 'starboard tack', with the wind on the starboard side.

Tack (Verb): To turn a sailing vessel through the wind (i.e. 'go about' so that the wind comes on the other side of the ship) by first turning her bows *into* the wind.

Taffrail: Rail at the stern.

Trucks: The small timber wheels for ship-board gun carriages.

Turn: Ropes are made fast around the belaying pins with figure-of-eight 'turns'.

Wear (Past tense Wore): The opposite to 'tack'; thus to put a sailing vessel about by first turning her bows *away* from the wind.

Windward: The side from which the wind is coming.

Yard: The spars across the masts to which the square sails (actually not square!) are attached; yardarms are the ends of the yards.

Index